A Complete

Single Moms

Everything You Need to
Know about Raising

Healthy, Happy Children
On Your Own

JANIS ADAMS

THE COMPLETE GUIDE TO FOR SINGLE MOMS: EVERYTHING YOU NEED TO KNOW ABOUT RAISING HEALTHY, HAPPY CHILDREN ON YOUR OWN

Copyright © 2011 Atlantic Publishing Group, Inc.
1405 SW 6th Avenue • Ocala, Florida 34471 • Phone 800-814-1132 • Fax 352-622-1875
Web site: www.atlantic-pub.com • E-mail: sales@atlantic-pub.com
SAN Number: 268-1250

Library of Congress Cataloging-in-Publication Data

Adams, Janis, 1967-
  A complete guide for single moms : everything you need to know about raising healthy, happy children on your own / by Janis Adams.
    p. cm.
Includes bibliographical references and index.
ISBN-13: 978-1-60138-397-6 (alk. paper)
ISBN-10: 1-60138-397-5 (alk. paper)
1. Single mothers--Life skills guides. 2. Single-parent families. 3. Parenting. I. Title.
HQ759.915.A33 2010
306.874'32--dc22
                        2010025453

PROJECT MANAGER: Amy Moczynski • amoczynski@atlantic-pub.com
PROOFREADER: Melissa Peterson • mpeterson@atlantic-pub.com
EDITORIAL ASSISTANT: Sarah Anne Beckman
PEER REVIEWER: Marilee Griffin • INTERIOR DESIGN: Rhana Gittens
FRONT & BACK COVER DESIGN: Jackie Miller • millerjackiej@gmail.com

Printed on Recycled Paper

We recently lost our beloved pet "Bear," who was not only our best and dearest friend but also the "Vice President of Sunshine" here at Atlantic Publishing. He did not receive a salary but worked tirelessly 24 hours a day to please his parents. Bear was a rescue dog that turned around and showered myself, my wife, Sherri, his grand-

parents Jean, Bob, and Nancy, and every person and animal he met (maybe not rabbits) with friendship and love. He made a lot of people smile every day.

We wanted you to know that a portion of the profits of this book will be donated to The Humane Society of the United States. *–Douglas & Sherri Brown*

The human-animal bond is as old as human history. We cherish our animal companions for their unconditional affection and acceptance. We feel a thrill when we glimpse wild creatures in their natural habitat or in our own backyard.

Unfortunately, the human-animal bond has at times been weakened. Humans have exploited some animal species to the point of extinction.

The Humane Society of the United States makes a difference in the lives of animals here at home and worldwide. The HSUS is dedicated to creating a world where our relationship with animals is guided by compassion. We seek a truly humane society in which animals are respected for their intrinsic value, and where the human-animal bond is strong.

Want to help animals? We have plenty of suggestions. Adopt a pet from a local shelter, join The Humane Society and be a part of

our work to help companion animals and wildlife. You will be funding our educational, legislative, investigative and outreach projects in the U.S. and across the globe.

Or perhaps you'd like to make a memorial donation in honor of a pet, friend or relative? You can through our Kindred Spirits program. And if you'd like to contribute in a more structured way, our Planned Giving Office has suggestions about estate planning, annuities, and even gifts of stock that avoid capital gains taxes.

Maybe you have land that you would like to preserve as a lasting habitat for wildlife. Our Wildlife Land Trust can help you. Perhaps the land you want to share is a backyard—that's enough. Our Urban Wildlife Sanctuary Program will show you how to create a habitat for your wild neighbors.

So you see, it's easy to help animals. And The HSUS is here to help.

2100 L Street NW • Washington, DC 20037 • 202-452-1100
www.hsus.org

Dedication

*To Colby, I am so very blessed to be
your mother. May you always ever be
a man after God's own heart.*

Table of Contents

Chapter 3: A Baby Is On The Way   47

Chapter 4: Adjustment for All –
Settling into Single Motherhood   71

Chapter 5:
The Other Half – My Child's Father   99

Chapter 6:
The Green Giant – Financial Affairs   137

Chapter 7: Sons & Daughters – Ages, Stages, Gender Roles, and Issues   167

Chapter 8:
Establishing Lifelines – Support Systems 195

Chapter 9: Leaving the Old Maid At Home –
Entering the World of Dating 229

Chapter 10: Somewhere Over the Rainbow- The Future   249

Conclusion: Single Mothers' Words of Wisdom 261

Appendix A: Pregnancy Preparedness Checklist 265

Appendix B: Resources   134

Bibliography   275

Author Biography   279

Index   281

Introduction

Being a single mom has been the most golden experience of my life. I consider it golden because while there have been trials and fiery times, it has produced the most valuable and lasting results in my life and in the life of my son. Just like gold is refined, so have I been refined and changed in a greater way because of having been a single mother. I would not be writing this book if my experience as a single mother had not been hopeless at the onset and then proved to be the greatest, most hope-filled experience of my life.

My job mothering is nearly done as my son is now an adult. Although I still can see the vestiges of the little boy with cerulean blue eyes, a single dimple, and a splatter of well-placed freckles, I know the man he has become is partially a product of my odyssey as a single mother.

A few months prior to turning 21, my son penned a letter to me that spoke of our experiences. In his looking back on his childhood, I was reminded of the truth of what it meant to be a single mother. His words, not all of which are included here, reminded me with candor what it means to be a single mother:

> "You have been one of the people in my life who has always been there for me. I had a very blessed childhood and growing up with you couldn't have been better. Of course, we had our rough patches in life, but us fighting through those made us stronger, never kept us down, and made us both better people. Not only are you my mom, you are my best friend."

As I read the entirety of the letter, I recalled the moments that were very difficult as a single mother raising a son. But it was those moments that not only molded my son into the man he is today, but also shaped me into a far better woman. Now that I am on the other side of single mothering, where the job is all but done, I see that I have learned so very much.

As a single mother just starting out, I wish there had been a book handed to me to guide my steps, provide encouragement, and remind me of those who had gone before me as successful single mothers. I hope these pages will give you hope, encouragement, and most of all pride in who you are as a mother and as a woman.

The Secret to Single Motherhood

It was through life's lessons that I learned the secret to single motherhood. The secret to being a single mother is that every situation is unique and every situation has unique options. In learning this invaluable lesson, I was freed to enjoy being a mother to my son in a way unique to our situation and in a style that best suited us.

The secret to single motherhood is that life is lived out by trial and error — with many errors. However, I am sure that my son would attest that within those errors contained the most important gift I could give my son: the knowledge that whoever he became, and however he became it, I would love him unequivocally without question. If I could not buy the sneakers he wanted or the latest electronic device, it not a reflection of my love for him. The secret to single motherhood is that material things do not make up for time spent with your child.

The secret to single mothering is that mistakes are part of the process. Do not attribute the mistakes that you make to the fact that you are parenting on your own — all parents, and I mean every darn one, makes mistakes.

The secret to single mothering is that there is no shame in raising a child on your own. Take pride; raising a child is no small feat, and doing it on your own is a Herculean accomplishment.

The secret to single mothering is that there are practical and helpful logistics afforded to a single mother. Help is out there, but first you must be willing to ask for help. Second, you must be willing to take the time to search out available options and offerings. An integral part of this secret is the realization that regardless of however "single" you are, the reality is you are not going to be parenting alone. There are numerous options for support for a mother parenting on her own. There is the support of family and friends, as well as uncountable numbers of resources now available to single mothers today. Children need to be woven into many lives, and just because you are parenting solo does not mean you are all the child needs in his or her life.

This book will serve as a guide through all the issues facing a single mother. This book will cover topics, including the way to successfully create a budget and eradicate debt from your life to how to handle the prospect of beginning to date. The book will explore gender issues and will focus on a how raising a boy differs from raising a girl, as well as how to find healthy role models for your children. As you read, you will also hear from other single mothers as they share their experiences throughout the pages of the book. Their testimonies can serve as both an encouragement when you think there is no one else who has been where you are and as a guide so that you can avoid mistakes others who have gone before you have already made.

My hope is that this book will lead you to realize the secrets of mothering your child in your own way, unique to your own situation.

Chapter 1

I'm a Single Mom — Now What?

You are now among a special group of women — single mothers. You are not alone. According to the U.S. Census Bureau, the national number of single mothers is rapidly rising. According to the U.S. Census Bureau, 36 percent of women ages 15 to 50 who gave birth in the past year were not currently married. According to Parents Without Partners, an organiza-

> *"None of us knows what the next change is going to be, what unexpected opportunity is just around the corner, waiting to change all the tenor of our lives."*
>
> *— Kathleen Thomson Norris*
> *American novelist*
> *July 16, 1880 – January 18, 1966*

tion designed to provide single parents and their children with an environment of support by offering regular meetings and activities, from 1990 to 2000, there was an increase of more than 3 million single mothers. Roughly translated, this means that by the year 2002, 23 percent of children lived with a single mother. A decade later, this figure continues to rise. The reality is there are many women who have thrived after becoming single mothers, and many children raised by single mothers have become successful adults.

For example, did you know that football greats Warrick Dunn and brothers Tiki and Ronde Barber were raised by single mothers? Baseball player Rickey Hendersen and Olympic gold medalist Michael Phelps were also raised by single mothers. Politician Alexander Haig and President Barack Obama also grew up in homes with a single mother. Comedian Bill Cosby, actress Julia Roberts, and singer Alicia Keys are the shining stars of single mothers. That is just to name a few people whose lives were shaped by single mothers.

You have the ability to become a strong, thriving single mother if you so choose. Whether you have become a single mother by choice — by artificial insemination, surrogacy, or adoption — or you have a become a single mother out of situations out of your control — whether as the result of divorce, widowhood, or the end of a relationship — the attitude you bring to mothering is entirely yours. You can cry, complain, and look at all the negatives to the situation, or you can choose to focus on the positives — whether they are clearly apparent to you at this juncture or not.

As the time for single mothering hits, it will be a time for some major lifestyle adjustments. As you step into your role as a single mother, you will be letting go of an old life to step into a new one. Even if you are ecstatic with joy about the upcoming arrival of a new child, leaving your previous lifestyle behind and starting a new life with shared accommodations can be daunting. Change of any kind in anyone's life can cause a period of mourning or grief over the lifestyle he or she once had, and this is normal and acceptable within healthy boundaries.

Many women, even when they made the choice to become a mother on their own, find letting go of their freedoms tinged by a wistfulness that often accompanies moving to a new place in life. One of the most important things you as a single mother will need to do is not focus on what you do not have, and instead, focus on the joys and blessings in life and the adventures single motherhood will inevitably bring you.

Accepting Your Circumstances

If circumstances out of your control have thrust single motherhood upon you, there is a natural grieving process that you must allow yourself to experience to become not only a healthy mother but a happy one too. The first step in this vital process is to offer yourself the understanding that grief is a natural and healthy response to the loss of something formerly in our lives or simply the loss of a lifestyle or status. It hurts, and it sometimes takes time to fully allow ourselves to feel the sadness, experience it, and move past it.

It is important as you embrace your new situation to keep talking. Find people who you can honestly share your feelings with. Think carefully about who you choose to share the intimacies of your life with, as personal details of your life need to be placed in the hearts and hands of those who will treasure information and keep it safe. Those listening need not even offer advice or solutions; they simply need to be available to listen. Often, we assume when we are hurting that we will be stronger if we are alone in our grief; this is untrue. Grief needs to be shared. There is no safety in pretending we are not grieving or experiencing a loss in our life.

As natural as it will be to think about your pre-single mommy lifestyle, you need to realize when you are dwelling too much on how things were, instead of embracing your present and anticipating your future. For some women, enduring difficult situations that place them into single motherhood, for example in the event of divorce or the death of a spouse, could mean that depression could take hold of their lives. Here are some warning signs to be aware of should you think you or another single mother you know may be experiencing symptoms of depression:

- Not being able to sleep or sleeping too much

- Not being able to stop eating or not eating and losing visible amounts of weight

- Extreme irritability

- Acute loss of concentration leaving you unable to accomplish daily tasks

- Acting in an overly manic, overly agitated state

- Feeling no hope, or often having thoughts of not wanting to live or suicidal tendencies

- Feelings of self-hatred or self-loathing

Should you experience any of these symptoms on an ongoing basis, you should seek help from a professional. Whether it be from your physician, therapist, or psychiatrist, it is important to reach out to a professional who can guide you to a healthy place — for both yourself and your children.

If you are a single mother by choice, you will not experience the grieving process other single mothers may experience. However, it does not mean that mothering will not come without significant adjustment. You may at times miss the simplicity of your life before making the choice to become a single mother. This is a normal reaction and nothing to be dismayed by or ashamed of. It is normal to have moments when it all seems overwhelming. All mothers face moments of doubt and uncertainty; the adjustment to motherhood is said to be the greatest change in a woman's life.

A Single Mother By Choice

Today, many women choose to become single mothers. The circumstances that lead them to this choice differ from one woman to another. One woman may choose to become a mother on her own because she is at a place in life where she would like to parent but has not met someone she wants to share her life with. Another woman may choose to bring a child into her heart and home because of the circumstances the child is in. Whatever leads each woman to her decision, becoming a single mother is an individual choice that is directed by the desires of the heart and head.

Single Mothers Speak

Tara Surowiec, mother of two

"My journey to becoming a single mom began when I was 27 years old and I received a call from a family member stating that my niece had been removed from her home and placed into a temporary foster home. I immediately considered requesting custody of my niece who was 8 years old at the time. I didn't share my thoughts with anyone initially.

I was single. I lived in a studio apartment, and I worked full time. So, I thought everyone would think it would be too much for me. First, I prayed. Then, I did extensive research and looked into the costs of after school care, talked to my employer about the opportunity for flexibility within my work schedule, and many other things that would be involved in raising a child while being single. I decided that I could partition off my studio apartment so we both had our separate areas (as bedrooms) and then if after six months she was still with me, I would move into a two-bedroom apartment.

When I first shared this with my mom, her main concern was that it would interfere with my finding a man who would want to not only marry me but be willing to take on a child. My response was always that we would be a package deal, and I felt strongly that if the right man were to come into my life — and my daughter's — that he would want and love us both.

After taking all of this into consideration, I went forward and entered a request for custody. After three months, I received physical custody, and then after about six months, I received legal custody. As much as people say this was a blessing to my niece, it was as much, if not more, of a blessing to me to have her in my life. There is not a single moment that I regret choosing to become a single mother."

However you came to be a single mother, you are going to need adapting skills. You are stepping into a new world that requires new navigation skills. Rest assured, this new world can and will be a great one if you choose for it to be.

Taking the Next Step

After you have embraced your new life as a single mom, you have to begin planning a future for yourself as well as your child or children. At this important juncture in your life, strategize to keep your thoughts moving in a positive direction. Think about the wonderful life that you alone have the opportunity to create for you and your child.

Your thought process at this juncture in your life will largely determine how the future for you and your child is written. No matter the situation in which you now find yourself, you are not alone. There are others who have gone before you who can serve as examples for you, and there will be those who come after you who you will one day serve as an example for. From this day forward, determine that you will not allow your circumstances to dictate your feelings. Determine to embrace the future that you will share with your child as a single mother.

There are about to be major changes in your life, and you need the resources to help you acclimate to this new environment. Regardless of the situations that brought you to single motherhood, successful single parenting revolves around a working plan. Planning, on all levels, allows you to move forward successfully. The first step on your journey as a successful, happy mother — whether you are starting this journey when you are pregnant or expecting a new child through adoption or surrogacy, or you have become a single mother through divorce or due to the loss of your child's father — is to decide who you want to tell about your new life as a single mother.

Your First Choice — To Tell or Not to Tell

You are in complete control of what information can and will be shared on your individual road to single motherhood. You are under no obligation to offer particulars or explanations as to the choices you have made and why you have made them. You also can feel free to not disclose information about the father of your child, should he still be a part of your life.

Many women struggle with this concept. There is a sense of obligation associated with a line of questioning and a feeling of guilt that is attached when we choose not to be entirely forthcoming when we are asked a question. However, do not feel pressured to share news with someone you deem does not have a right to your personal information. Your approach to motherhood as a single woman is a private and personal decision, the details of which do not have to be disclosed. So are the details surrounding your becoming a single mother by divorce or because of the end of any relationship or because you have chosen to become a mother on your own.

This ability to say "No" and create boundaries are attributes a single mother must acquire early as she endeavors to succeed in her new role. It is absolutely acceptable to say "No" or politely decline offering more details about your personal life. Learning to say "No" is a process that takes time and practice. Do not be too hard on yourself if you feel cornered during a conversation and feel you divulged more than you would have wished to share. Simply learn from the experience so you will be better prepared for the next time. Once you have availed yourself of the ability to say "No," the next step in preparing for single motherhood is planning.

Planning for Change

The most important item a single woman will need is a plan, because a plan is the best and most beneficial way to move forward in your new life as a mom. No two mothers have the same story of how they came to be a single parent, so no two plans will be the same. Your plan will also have to be altered along the way to meet you and your child's ever-changing needs. You will need to have short- and long-term plans, both of which have to be realistic.

Single Mothers Speak

Colene Carpenter, mother of one

"While it is not always easy, I like that I get to make all the decisions for raising my son on my own. I like knowing that through careful planning, I am accomplishing the things that I want to as a mother. I feel proud when others see my son and tell me what a great job I am doing raising my son on my own."

Creating short-term and long-term plans

To begin creating a short-term plan, it is helpful to make a list of all your and your child's immediate needs, which include housing; having adequate child care if and when you must be absent from your child; groceries; and more. Once you have assessed what your immediate needs are, determine if you can successfully meet them.

As you formulate this plan, remember to overestimate your needs rather than underestimate them so you will reach far fewer crisis management points within your plan. If you minimize your expenses and an unexpected financial need arises, you may not have the money to cover this unforeseen expense. Be sure to plan proactively instead of reactively.

With that in mind, it is more important than ever to create a financial plan. One of the reasons to create a plan is that it will ensure you and your child will live a more comfortable life now and in the future. And while it may seem a bit forward thinking to plan for a child's financial future, it is not. Setting a financial plan in motion has motivated people to greater economic success. This financial strategizing will include short-term budgeting and long-term financial planning. *This topic will be discussed later in Chapter 5 and will cover the best possible financial scenario for you and your child.* With this in mind, it is good to begin at the earliest point possible to strategize on the best and most economical plan for your child's birth and future.

To start planning proactively, begin making lists. First, list the needs that you can address without changing anything in your current lifestyle. These may include housing, groceries, utilities, and transportation. Next, list the needs that can be addressed with a bit of modification to your present lifestyle. For example, consider whether you can change a spare bedroom into a nursery or trade in your two-seat sports car for a car that will accommodate a child safety seat. Lastly, make a list of those things that will require definite changes whether in monetary resources, time, or lifestyle arrangements. Some changes that most likely may require a significant change are providing day care for your child, making adjustments in your work schedule, and adjusting health insurance coverage. Begin to make a plan to address these issues in their order of importance.

Items of pressing importance can include things like purchasing a car seat prior to the arrival of the baby or perhaps trading in or purchasing a different car if you currently have a sporty two-door model. Also, getting a crib and making sure health care will be in place for your baby when he or she arrives are a few ideas of things that must be taken note of before the birth of your baby. Those items on your list that need to be addressed prior to the arrival of a baby should be placed on a page of priority items, and you should make a time table as to when each item must be attended to. *See Appendix A for a list of items that will help you prepare for your pregnancy.*

In prioritizing you and your child's need and wants, try to put your emotions aside and rely on your logic. In an effort to recognize the importance or the priority of these items, ask yourself what you need or what your child needs. Obviously, the first needs you should address are housing, food, transportation, and child care. One significant detail that is often overlooked in setting your top priority items is the need for health insurance. Health insurance may, at first, seem like a negligible need; however, having a child means having health insurance is imperative. It is important to note one illness while uninsured can wipe out all your monetary resources in one fell swoop and can leave staggering figures of debt.

Another important decision to make is what to do regarding extracurricular activities your child may want to become involved in. While these activities may be important, they are not vital to the very existence of your child. For example, playing a local town sport instead of playing on a club traveling team, which requires large sums of money to participate, is something that should be taken into consideration. Or perhaps reconsider purchasing the latest trend in sneakers for your child and instead opt for a cheaper brand simply to stay within a budget. Those things that are not requisite to living must be placed at a lower level of priority. While this may be painful for both you and your child to adjust to, it is important to not deplete your monetary resources.

While at times this may be difficult, making these types of choices for yourself and your child can teach lasting values to him or her as he or she matures. Instead of making these decisions difficult for yourself and your child, create ways and systems to save money so that you can earn the opportunities to have the things you want. For example, if you are in the habit of stopping for dinner at a restaurant a few nights week, cut back. Portion out the money you are saving by eating at home. Consider saving money — an important task — and then when a sufficient amount is saved, allow yourself or your child to indulge in a predetermined want (in this case, it could be a night out to your favorite restaurant).

As you list your and your child's needs, make a list of options for meeting each of the needs. Each item on your plan should have more than one option beside it. For example, when considering housing, think of location options, which may include the option of sharing housing with another single mother or with a friend, which can reduce cost and create a support system.

While you are establishing short- and long-term goals and planning ways to meet them, there is another plan a single mother must always keep in mind — a plan for some type of relaxation or fun. This plan is important to the health and happiness of you and your child. Pack some snacks or a lunch and take a trip to the park. You can meet up with some friends for coffee or for an afternoon out to do some window shopping. This break a single mother needs to afford herself does not require spending money, just a respite of time. Allow yourself to set aside your worries and your planning and take a huge breath. Taking a one- or two-day break from planning not only allows you to refresh yourself, but it also gives you a fresh look at your plan when you return to your list.

While you are planning, it is important to recognize it is a good and healthy thing to ask for help when you need it. Many mothers enter into the thinking and planning process and say to themselves, "If I need to ask for help, I am not doing a good job as a mother." This is an erroneous thought and one that should be dispelled immediately. Help is necessary for every good mother, whether she is single or married; make a choice to ask for help when needed. One of the best ways a mother can receive help is through a support system of family and friends that she can turn to for assistance and love.

Chapter 2

Finding Support for Your New Lifestyle

Pregnancy as a single mother can be planned or unplanned; either way, a baby is a joyous event. Regardless of the circumstances surrounding the pregnancy, this momentous occasion should be counted as a blessed one. Each step should be marked with planning and with hope,

"It was only a sunny smile, And cost little in the giving, But like the morning light, It scattered the night, And made the day worth living."

— Anonymous

excitement, and eager anticipation. Pregnancy is a time for forward thinking. From beginning to end, a mother does not want to look back and wish she enjoyed her pregnancy more because during that time she was focused on the struggles instead of the joy.

Whether you are carrying a baby to term yourself, working with a surrogate, or bringing a child into your home through adoption or a host of other scenarios, there should be no room for the stigma of guilt or shame because you are parenting as a single woman. If single motherhood is brought to you by way of a newborn, there will be those who may feel entitled to ask quite a few questions. Many times, these questions are inappropriate and do not necessarily deserve or require you to answer them.

Obviously, not all women become single mothers through pregnancy or adoption. Often, women will experience the end of a relationship or the death of a spouse, leaving them the sole caretaker for their child or children. Regardless of the situation that led you to become a single mother, you will inevitably realize you will need to turn to someone for help and support at times. With that in mind, it is imperative that you determine who you will be able to turn to for support in the time ahead. While monetary issues will prove to be of great importance in the coming months and years, even more vital is the support system that you must define and establish for yourself.

Don't Be Afraid To Ask

In the next section, the focus will be on choosing who you will turn to for support. However, before you can turn to someone for support, you must be willing to ask for it. Asking for help by reaching out for support is often difficult for anyone; this is not unique to a single mother. Pride will often step in the way and prevent us from reaching out for help from those who can provide it. As a mother, you will learn that pride goes out the window as you parent. Our children will do things unintentionally — and intentionally — that embarrass us. It is a part of life. The reality is pride should not control your life as a mother. When you are in need of support, you have to put your own feelings aside and think of what is best for your children. This is not always easy, but it is imperative that you learn to make this choice. If choosing to ask for help is difficult, it will be even more important to choose whom you ask for help wisely.

Who Will You Turn to for Support?

Unfortunately, many women opt to isolate themselves as they are on their way to single motherhood. Even when becoming a single mother is a choice, from the beginning, there can be apprehensions as to whether to share the news. This reaction of social isolation stems from the concerns of how people will react to your new circumstances, and anticipating rejection can cause avoidance.

What a single mother needs to do at this point is take ownership of her situation and circumstances. If you do not, you will lose a sense of control of the situation, which is an important foundation for building your and your child's future. The reality is that no one will agree with you and your choices all the time; this is true for everyone, not just for single mothers. Do not prejudge people's reactions, but instead, allow them the opportunity to be a part of the new life you are creating.

Part of finding support is recognizing yourself as your own support system. You may be asking yourself, "How can I be my own support system?" Choosing to look at your life in a positive light is the first and foremost way you can support yourself. Keep in mind the shadow you cast on your circumstances largely determines the attitude with which others will perceive your circumstances. If you are negative about what is occurring around you, the people around you will pick up on this. Choose to see, feel, and experience the joy in your daily living. This is a choice you will be making, both for yourself and your child.

Of course, if you find that anyone you are relating to on an ongoing basis brings a negative attitude or approach that seems to be crippling your relationship with them, it is healthy to create some distance between you and that person. As a single mother who is about to embark on the greatest challenge of a lifetime, it is best to surround yourself with your own personal pep squad. One of the first places you can look to for support is your family members.

Single Mothers Speak

Brenda Mehrkar-Asl, mother of four

"Without question, a single mother cannot survive without people to support her. My family — and certain friends — provide unconditional support to me and my kids. Without them, I would never have survived. I needed their support, whether it was just to listen to me, help me out when I was overwhelmed, or give me advice or direct me to resources, I needed support. A single mother cannot hope to survive unless she allows people to offer their support to her."

Figuring Out Where Family Fits

Family can play a large part in our lives — both for the positive and the negative. The role that family will play in the raising of your child is important to determine early on, keeping in mind this dynamic can be adjusted as time progresses.

First, do not make any assumptions about what any member of your family will do or say. Discuss your needs with your family members and determine whether they are willing to be a part of the plan you are making for you and your child. Whether you are becoming a single mother of a newborn or an older child, candidly share your needs with trusted family members. Then, openly discuss how and in what way your family can meet these needs.

However, do not assume your family members will be able to do everything you may ask of them. For example, do not presume that because your mother is at home and does not work that she will be a willing babysitter for your child. If your sister has young children that go to the same school as your child, do not think she will willingly take your child to school and watch him or her after school until you return home from work. While your family may be willing to support you in your life as a single mother, do not make the mistake of thinking they will be able to do everything you may need them to do.

If you do have family members who are willing and able to assist you, thank them for their support and clearly define what role they will play. Allow yourself to clearly understand their intentions, and then make it apparent the ways you expect them to provide support for you and your child. It is important for you as a mother to be proactive rather than reactive because being proactive spares people's feelings in the long run. Clearly communicate your needs, wants, and desires. It is important to define what support a person will provide on an ongoing basis so no one will feel unfairly taken advantage of.

If you are fortunate enough, family can provide their time, emotional support, and financial help along the way. Often, a family member proves to be a generous helper when needs arise for a single mother. However, a family member cannot be considered an ATM, supplying cash as needed. While many families willingly contribute financially to raising a child, it is important to define these contributions. If they are loans, repayment terms need to be stipulated clearly early on. Monetary issues can contribute to long-standing issues between friends and family members, so it is best to clearly establish the rules of the lending game from the beginning.

After your family, your friends may also be able to provide emotional support as you adapt to solo parenting.

All Types of Friends

Help often comes by way of friends; they can be one of a single mother's greatest resources for support, encouragement, a night out, and so much more. You should approach your friends the same way that you would approach family members because it is unfair to assume friends will instantly become caretakers along with you. It will be encouraging when you find friends who are willing to offer help to you and your child or children, but do not think all your friends will automatically jump at the chance to assist you.

There are all types of friends in our lives. There are the friends we can call in the middle of the night to rescue us; the friends we choose as a shopping partner because they always tell the truth about how we look; or the friends we meet for dinner every now and again but would never dream of calling if we have a bad day. Each of your friends will play a role of substance in your life. The group of friends you meet for coffee will provide a much needed break, and the friends who are willing to stay up with you through the night with a colicky baby will bring their unique brand of support. All your different kinds of friends are of great and valuable consequence in a single mother's world.

It will also be important for you to continue making new friends while you are raising your child. Instead of skipping out on a get-together at your child's day care, sports event, or school, you should make an effort to attend. Get involved with any of these activities because you will meet other people who have at least one thing in common with you — children the same age as your child or children, which is a starting point for forging some new relationships. Another way to meet other parents is to stick around at drop-off time for your child's activity, because many times, other parents will linger and talk after leaving their children.

No matter the way you choose to find connections during this new time in your life, the important thing is you are able to connect with someone. This is not the time to become an introvert and stay home alone. This is an exciting time, with many new and unique possibilities. Single motherhood can be like a trip to a new place for the first time; it can be an exciting adventure marked by new events and different sights and filled with friends, both those you are already know and the new ones you have yet to meet.

Regardless what role a friend or family member plays in our life, boundaries need to be clearly defined. Sometimes, the support friends and family think they are giving you will end up causing more harm than good. This can happen if family or friends take it upon themselves to talk badly about your ex, should he still be in the picture. You should clearly state you do not want to focus on bashing your former partner but would rather pay attention to the family you are creating on your own. While at first it may seem like bashing the father helps support the mother, it erodes and deteriorates the relationship between the two parents and will prove to be anything but supportive. It might feel good momentarily, but it will not ultimately bring good or healthy results.

Deciding whether to involve your child's father

Another important question you need to answer will be what part of the support system the father of your child will play. What roles will he play in your life and the life of your child or children? While many people will gladly weigh in on the answer to this question, the only person who can best answer these questions is you.

If you have chosen to become a single mother and the paternal figure is currently absent from the scenario, will he later be present for the life of the child? Or, is there a possibility that at a later date you believe that he may be part of the parenting process? At the onset of becoming a single mother, unless you have become a single mother through anonymous donor insemination, adoption, surrogacy, or widowhood, the role of the father of your child must be defined. This definition most surely can be amended and the logistics revisited throughout the coming years as age and circumstances change, but for the time being, an understanding needs to be reached.

Whether your child's father is going to play a role in your child's life is a big decision. Going into this decision-making process, be sure to remember his reaction to your pregnancy or to your child should in no way affect your feelings about the child  you have chosen to raise on your own.

While you will be the one deciding what role the father will ultimately have in your son or daughter's life, it is important to allow your child's father to express his intentions regarding participating in your child's life. Does he plan to play an ongoing part in the daily life of your son or daughter? How involved does he want to be? Will he provide not only emotional support but financial support as well? These are all questions that need to be directly answered.

For the emotional well-being of you and your child, it is important to know from the beginning what you can expect from your child's father. At this point, it is often wise to consult legal counsel. Having ground rules that are clearly defined creates a more stable environment for everyone involved. A legal agreement can save many verbal disagreements in the future and create healthy and clearly defined boundaries that all parties can follow. *You can read more information about working with your child's father in Chapter 5.*

Involving a child's birth mother or surrogate

Similar to the questions and the thought process associated with defining the role of the father is deciding what role a birth mother or a surrogate mother should play in your child's life. These questions are ones that you as the mother are entitled to answer, but they do not have to be answered immediately. It is important to give yourself the opportunity to think through this issue and allow yourself the freedom — without pressure — to revisit this issue as needs and life dynamics change over time.

Single Mothers Speak

Tara Surowiec, mother of two

"There was a delicate balance in including my daughter's natural mother in our lives. Initially, I had to make the choices of what was best for my daughter. As my daughter has gotten older, I have given her more and more say in relating to her mother. Now that she is an adult, she defines how that relationship plays out in her life and how it will in the future."

Some adoption or surrogate relationships continue long after the birth of a child where the people involved continue to have close contact and relate to each other on an ongoing basis. This choice is up to you. Instead of feeling daunted by this decision, relax in the freedom that every relationship proves to be unique. As a mother, you may feel close to the birth mother or the surrogate and you may desire ongoing contact. However, other dynamics of the relationship can prove strenuous. If this happens to you, you may want to keep a distance between your child and his or her birth family.

In thinking through the needs of your child, it is important to recognize that your child will develop an identity and a definition of themselves. Whether you gave birth to your child, your child is adopted, from a surrogate, or from a sperm donor, as your child ages, he or she will have a variety of questions and concerns.

All children have questions regarding where they came from. Even at a young age, they begin to want to create a history for themselves. They want to know the circumstances surrounding their arrival in your life — no matter what or how that arrival came to be. These stories create a foundation for their knowledge of who they are. Some questions are playful while other questions can prove to be quite serious. Questions can range from "How tall is my dad?" to "Do I look like my birth mother?" or even "Did you and my dad split up because of me?" Have no fear; these questions are healthy and normal and are related to a child coming to understanding of who they are and where they come from. Kids today are taking a more active role in defining who they are by understanding their heritage. These questions in no way reflect on you as a mother or your parenting.

Making your own choices

An important question to ask yourself is, "What is good for my child in *our* situation? What will ultimately prove to be best for my child?" It is important to remember you should answer these questions in the most honest way possible.

Do not let these decisions about who you should turn to burden or overwhelm you. These decisions, while important, can be reworked should you see that certain people are not beneficial or healthy for you, your child, or both. If you recognize that you — or your child — will benefit from the support or the care that any of these people can offer, you should accept this support or care if it does not in any way jeopardize the emotional health of you or your child. As a mother, you should not feel uncomfortable in receiving help or financial aid simply because another mother handled a similar situation differently or did not need help in a certain area. Do not feel obligated to follow in the steps another mother has chosen to go; choose what is best for you and your child and your situation.

The following is a list of some avenues you can traverse as resources to help you and your child have your basic needs met. *You can find a more comprehensive list in Appendix B.*

- The Supplemental Nutrition Assistance Program, formerly called the Food Stamp Program, helps low-income families receive nutrition assistance. For more information about the program, visit **www.ers.usda. gov/briefing/SNAP** or call 1-800-221-5689.

- National School Lunch Program (NSLP) provides lunches during the academic year and also offers food programs during the months when school is not in session. Visit their website at **www.fns.usda.gov/cnd/ lunch**.

- Feeding America (**http://feedingamerica.org**) provides assistance to more than 37 million low-income people each year, including more than 14 million children.

Other Sources for Support

Support can come from other sources than family and friends and can prove to be just as valuable. Some examples of other places you should look for support include:

- **Community organizations** — These places also have a wealth of untapped resources. Often, these organizations offer their resources for free, and as a single mother, it is imperative you stash away your pride and accept assistance in any way that will benefit you or your child. There is no shame in getting help, no matter what form it comes in, and single mothers should take advantage of any assistance they may be able to receive; a single mother (or any parent for that matter) can never be too frugal in today's economy.

- **Other parents** — Parents of your child's friends may prove to be good resources. When another parent is picking up his or her child from an event, if something has created a last-minute dilemma, it is often not a problem to ask that parent to pick up your child as well. You can easily return the favor by offering to pick up their child the following week. Often, this can lead to a winning situation for both parents by cutting the driving in half. Sharing clothing that your child or other children have outgrown is another way to share resources and cut costs. Oftentimes, children who are experiencing growth spurts outgrow their clothing before it even shows wear. Ask other parents if they would not mind giving you any items their children can no longer wear, and offer the same thing to other parents of children younger or smaller than yours. By doing this, you can instate a reciprocally beneficial system.

- **Churches** — Often, churches have programs already in place that provide food, clothing, and various types of assistance for single mothers in need. Churches often work together to provide these services and a host of other ones to single mothers free of charge. For example, some churches offer after school programs for children of single mothers and/or low-cost babysitting or child care services.

- **Support groups** — Help can also come from single mother/single parent support groups. These groups will generally provide assistance by providing resources for group members. As well, they are usually a good place to go for local programs created to aid and support single parents. Help can come to the single mother in any combination of manner or means; it simply needs to reached for when needed.

The fundamental tool to success as a single mother is the knowledge of when to ask for help. An even greater tool is having the security to be able to reach out and accept help from others without feeling as if you are not doing your job as a mother.

Where to turn for health insurance

Whether you are bringing a new baby home from the hospital or you are now going to be raising your children without their father in the picture, one of the first things you need to figure out is what you are going to do about health insurance. Children of all ages get sick very easily, and if you have a newborn, there will be countless doctor visits you and your little one will need to attend. Not having health insurance will place significant strain on your budget, especially if you are not receiving financial support from the father of your child.

Single mothers are afforded options for insurance other than traditional plans employers offer. As a part of the U.S. Department of Health and Human Services, Medicaid — a government-operated insurance provider — offers medical benefits for those who qualify. As a part of the Children's Health Insurance Program, Medicaid offers plans for children who are not covered by their parent's insurance. Services include well-baby visits to the pediatrician, emergency and sick visits, low-cost or no-cost prescriptions, as well as dental and optical plans for those who qualify. Although the Medicaid program is ultimately guided by rules the federal government established, state governments control specifics as to eligibility qualifications. State governments not only determine who is eligible but also what benefits local Medicaid programs will cover. For more information on Medicaid-sponsored programs, go to the Medicaid website at **www.cms.hhs.gov/home/medicaid.asp**.

Private health insurance is another avenue for coverage that a single mother should not bypass when looking for options. A useful tool is the website eHealthInsurance Services, Inc. (**www.ehealthinsurance.com**), which offers visitors the opportunity to view and compare insurance providers' rates. It also gives a detailed description of what each provider's plan offers and an explanation of the different levels of insurance each provider offers. By using this site, or a site like it, you can find the plan that best suits your circumstances.

It is important to search out these options and understand their offerings.

If you are in the middle of divorce proceedings, it is important that you know your rights in regard to maintaining health benefits for your child and yourself. Different insurance companies have different policies, and a written explanation of the practices of the policy should be obtained prior to making any decisions or changes in the existing policy.

There are also various government-subsidized programs offering insurance plans that single mothers are afforded the opportunity to take advantage of. The Department of Social Services should be your first stop when considering these types of programs, as they are the largest and most far-reaching organization. Type in "Department of Social Services" into an online search engine and search the websites by state — each state has its own social services branch. By visiting the website of your local social service branch, you can complete an online application or you can call and request one. As well, consult your local health department as it may be able to provide additional information. In most cases, proof of income must be provided, and various other forms of paperwork and submissions need to be made before your specific case can be considered. If you do not meet the requirements to receive federally subsidized insurance, check with local insurance agencies to know your options.

Another example of a program you can utilize is the Women, Infant, and Children (WIC) program. WIC is a federally subsidized food and nutrition service and is available to women and children who qualify due to economic hardship. Services WIC offers are available to pregnant, nursing, and non-nursing women; infants; and children up to the age of 5. WIC provides vouchers for the purchase of milk, juice, eggs, breakfast cereal, cheese, bread, fish, legumes, fruits, vegetables, infant formula, and peanut butter. If you choose, soy products may be substituted for dairy items if you or your child is lactose intolerant. As well, there are alternatives that allow you to purchase whole wheat; for example oatmeal, brown rice, or whole wheat tortillas may be purchased instead.

Now that you have established a good support system to help you on your journey of solo parenting, you should consider how to prepare yourself in the event you are pregnant. *If you are not pregnant, you can skip to Chapter 4 to learn more about settling into your new role as head of household.*

Chapter 3

A Baby Is On The Way

If you are expecting a child and raising your future son or daughter as a single mommy, after you have established a good support system, you must begin looking for health care options and providers.

> "Women know the way to rear up children (to be just). They know a simple, merry, tender knack of tying sashes, fitting baby-shoes, and stringing pretty words that make no sense..."
>
> – Elizabeth Barrett Browning
> English poet
> March 6, 1806 – June 29, 1861

Choosing Physicians and Medical Care

Once your insurance is in place, it is time to find an obstetrician or gynecologist to care for your needs during the coming months. Choosing a doctor to deliver your baby should be a carefully thought out decision; the doctor you choose should be one who believes in the approach to medical care most closely to your own.

An obstetrician gynecologist, or an ob/gyn, is a doctor who provides a variety of women's health services. An obstetrician provides care before, during, and immediately after childbirth. Many doctors — those who practice both obstetrics and gynecology — choose a dual role in women's care, which means that following the birth of your child, you will be able to continue seeing the doctor who served as your obstetrician to address your continuing health care needs.

When preparing to find a doctor who will assist you in the birth of your child, one of the first things that you should take into consideration is whether you will be more comfortable during the birthing process with a male or a female at your side. The next thing you should do is ask yourself what kind of approach you want to take for the birth and future care for your child. Do you want a traditional approach? Do you want to pursue a holistic (an approach that considers the physical, the mental, and the spiritual as equally important to address) or alternative methods of medicine? The answers to these questions and similar ones can provide a basis for narrowing down your choices of ob/gyns.

Before visiting a doctor to choose the correct ob/gyn, ensure they take your insurance plan. Most insurance providers will supply a list of doctors who accept their plans. If you are unable to find this information from your insurance provider, call the doctor's office and ask the receptionist whether the office accepts your insurance.

Once you have chosen a doctor to assist you with your pregnancy and delivery, it is important for you to have a doctor, either a pediatrician or family practitioner, in place for your child. A pediatrician can prove to be a great resource and an invaluable support system when raising a child on your own. No matter your route to becoming a single mother, it is vital you have an established relationship with a pediatrician.

It is important to take time to choose a pediatrician who will best fit your needs and your approach to parenting and health care. Ask yourself what is important to you in a health care provider. Here are some questions you may want to ask yourself to help find a physician who will most appropriately meet your needs:

- Do you want to have the same doctor each time you make an appointment?

- Would you be comfortable with a multi-doctor practice? Multi-doctor practices have more than one attending physician located within the same office system. As a patient within a multi-doctor practice, you are not guaranteed to see the same physician at each visit. When you visit a multi-doctor practice, the doctor who is on call or in the office at the time will assist you. Multi-doctor practices have a number of doctors housed in the same location whose schedules evolve on a rotating basis.

- If a holistic approach to medicine is important to you, does the pediatrician offer this?

- How far is the office located from where you live?

Most of these questions can be answered by a simple call to the doctor's office and requesting to speak with the office manager or the nurse's assistant.

One of the best resources for finding a pediatrician is asking other mothers who their pediatrician is and if they are happy with the doctor and the services the office staff and nurses provide. You can also ask your ob/gyn if they have any recommendations. Often your ob/gyn will provide general information on a few pediatricians they refer their patients' children to. However, a doctor's views of the pediatricians he or she refers are not as candid as another mother's viewpoint might be.

Comprise a list of pediatricians who meet your qualifications, and then make an appointment to speak with them in person. Get a feel for who they are and how comfortable you will feel relating to them on an ongoing basis. It is important to feel that you can trust your pediatrician and that they are someone you can easily approach. Should health concerns arise — and they often do with children — you want your child's pediatrician to be an approachable resource.

Now that medical care and doctors are in place, the next step in preparing for a new child is to decide who will be involved in the pregnancy.

When Expecting, What to Expect

Pregnancy oftentimes brings up many questions and these questions most often should first be directed to your ob/gyn. Your chosen doctor will be able to help you discern what is healthy and what is not, what you should be doing for yourself, and what you should be abstaining from for the best health of your baby. Your ob/gyn will also provide detailed information on each stage of pregnancy and what is to be expected.

As you near the end of your pregnancy, many issues will present themselves that need be addressed, and these decisions should be made without pressure from outside sources. Some questions you may want to ask yourself are:

- Who do you feel most comfortable with? Remember to ask yourself if you would be comfortable with having this person see you disrobed during the birthing process.

- Who do you want with you when the baby first comes home? It is important to have help of some kind so that you are able to get proper rest.

- Do you want to or can you afford private nursing care?

- What will you do in the event that you have an unplanned caesarean section and initially need on-site, at-home help?

For some single mothers, preparing for the birth of their child means considering who will be a part of the birthing process, which includes taking childbirth classes to the actual birth. For other mothers who are adopting or having a surrogate carry their child, it means who will provide support immediately after their infant is placed in their arms. These are important decisions and should be given ample consideration before deciding who you want around you in these most important first days, weeks, and months.

After a doctor is chosen, the next step in the process is to decide your childbirth options. Speak candidly with your ob/gyn. Relay your desires and how you envision your ideal birthing experience; you should even share any fears that you may have. Today, mothers have a great deal more options than in the past. Doing a bit of research will give you a better idea of what setting would most fit your desires for the birthing process. Take these things into consideration, as well as the financial outlay necessary before making a decision.

Some questions that mothers may ask themselves can range from deciding where they would like to give birth to what makes the birthing process the most comfortable for them. Does the doctor practice at the hospital that you like best or that is closest to you, or will you have to go to a different location from the one you are most familiar with? How much medical intervention do you want? Another important decision an expecting mother will have to make is where she wants to give birth.

Birthing Locations

There are three common options for your birthing experience: a hospital, a birthing center, or at home.

During the 20th century, there was a sharp decline in the popularity of home births, due to the fact that hospitals can more effectively address complications associated with childbirth than home births that go unassisted by a medical professional. While some women may still prefer to give birth at home, most mothers choose to give birth in a hospital, both because extensive medical care is available on site should the need arise and due in part to the fact that nearly all hospitals now offer birthing suites designed to make the mother feel as if she is giving birth at home. Rooms are now decorated in a feminine way and machines are hidden behind furniture-looking enclosures. Birthing suites now often include a bathtub or whirlpool tub, easy chairs, and sometimes even a small kitchenette. For these reasons, mothers are opting for a birthing suite that can provide immediate medical attention available verses the home birth.

In a hospital experience, the birth takes place at the hospital where your doctor is affiliated in a controlled and regulated environment. Full medical intervention is available should you need it during the labor and delivery process.

Birthing centers

A birthing center traditionally has all the standard medical equipment a hospital will have, but it caters only to women who are pregnant or giving birth. Birthing centers have to follow regulations and meet specific medical standards governed by state licensing, but these differ from state to state, making the approach offered different from one location to the next. Centers must be state licensed and should be accredited by the National Associations of Childbearing Centers. Also, midwives employed by the birthing center should be licensed. For more information on the accreditation process, go to the American Association of Birth Center's website at **www.birthcenters.org**.

Birthing centers can only service patients who have been deemed in good general health and are at low risk for a complicated pregnancy outcome. These centers must comply with clinical records statutes, documenting all procedures and services provided to a patient.

In terms of accommodations, some birthing centers have private suites that would simulate a bedroom while still having medical equipment available during the birthing process. As well, there are hospitals that have birthing centers that are affiliated with them so if an extreme medical need arises, attention can be given speedily.

Home births

Another example of a birthing location is at home. Home births are often assisted by a midwife or a doula — a professional trained in the art of childbirth or as a labor support companion. While a midwife or doula is trained to assist in the birthing process, these professionals are not medical doctors as an ob/gyn is. A doula will provide his or her services for an at-home birth or will also assist in the birthing process at a hospital. A doula may prove to be a viable option for a single mother who needs support during the birthing process but does not have a friend or family available to come to the child's delivery. In choosing the services of a doula — verses opting to use a midwife — a mother will receive not only care during the birthing process, but also care during the postpartum adjustment period. A midwife's services are primarily aimed at aiding the mother during the birth, while a doula offers more comprehensive and long-term care for the mother and child.

A doula's services can last up to a few weeks or a few months postpartum, depending on the mother's needs and wishes. Some women feel that they need the guidance and support of their doulas as they transition from stage to stage in the first days, weeks, and, if need be, months.

You doctor or local hospital can provide you with a list of local midwives and doulas. Many times, the midwives and doulas a hospital refers are in fact affiliated with that hospital. Having a midwife or a doula that has an established relationship with a hospital is important in the event complications arise during the birthing process.

Choosing a midwife or a doula is a decision that takes research to ensure you and your child will be receiving the best care possible. You will also want to choose someone who you can feel entirely safe and comfortable with, as they will be sharing one of the most intimate moments of your life. Do not feel uncomfortable interviewing more than one or many people for this position; make sure you find the person that best suits you. As well, ask for a list of those women who have previously used the person's services so that you can contact them as a reference.

Labor coaches and partners

Nearly all mothers choose to have a "labor coach" on hand to encourage them and guide them through the labor process. Choosing a coach is a very personal matter, and your coach should be someone who you feel will prove to be your greatest encourager and your most treasured ally. They must be able to be ready on a moment's notice, for as we all know, the arrival of a baby is not usually a scheduled event. While it is most common to choose a family member or a close friend to serve as a labor coach, there are those who choose to contract a professional for this purpose. Most medical practices have information on people who provide this service.

Another option open to mothers-to-be who do not choose a family member or friend for a coach is hiring a labor partner. A labor partner is a trained professional who will provide guidance and reassurance through the entire birthing process. A labor partner is not a medical professional, but simply someone who has been trained to meet all of a birthing mother's needs. Some labor partners are more expensive than others due to their medical background — former nurses and labor and delivery specialists often choose to become labor partners due to the deeper, ongoing relationships they can develop with clients. An ob/gyn or local birthing center should be able to provide a list of labor coaches or labor partners, and there are also websites that will provide this information. One such website is Dona International (**www.dona. org**), which can guide you through finding the right person to assist you through the birthing process.

Regardless of what birthing option you choose, you will still need to plan adequately in the months leading up to the birth. Plans should include who to call at the onset of labor and how you will get to the hospital. What will you do in the event of an unscheduled caesarean birth? Who will be with you through labor? These and other similar questions should be answered prior to the last month of pregnancy.

After you have made the necessary preparations and brought your new child into the world, it is time to prepare yourself for bringing home a baby.

Bringing Baby Home

When you bring your baby home from the hospital, a birthing center, or an adoption location, you are required to use a car seat. Hospital officials are known to check a car before fully discharging baby and new mom. Many adoption agencies have also taken to this practice when releasing a newborn.

At home, a mother will need a bed or bassinet for the baby to sleep in. A bassinet is used from birth to about 4 months old, or when a baby begins to roll over on his or her own. A bassinet can prove quite handy as you can easily move it from one room to another to have the newborn close to you. A Moses basket, although less sturdy, is a more portable version of the bassinet that allows a mother to carry the bed from room to room.

A baby bed or a crib is another option for a newborn. These tend to be stationary and can serve the child into his or her toddler years. Traditionally, a crib is more expensive than a bassinet, but it offers greater stability and more years of use. As well, after using a traditional crib, the mattress can be used to transition a toddler to a regular bed. Low to the ground bed frames that employ the former crib mattress are easy to find in most baby stores and many furniture stores as well.

Along with your choice of sleeping accommodations for your new little one, you will need what is commonly referred to as a layette. A layette is all basic baby clothing items a newborn will need. Some of these items include:

- Blankets
- Burp cloths
- Booties
- Hats
- Undershirts
- Onesies
- Caps
- Buntings
- Baby wraps
- Bibs
- Towels and wash cloths
- Cloth diapers

A trip down any baby aisle at a local drug store will give you an idea of all the basics you will need to have those first few days. A thermometer, a tube of ointment for diaper rash, and all the supplies necessary for changing baby — diapers, wipes, and lotion — are just a few of the items you should have on hand for your child. Prior to purchasing or administering any type of over-the-counter medication for your newborn, consult with his or her pediatrician. Newborns cannot be given regular strength children's or adult dosages of medications at any time.

Bottles are also needed whether you have chosen to breast-feed your newborn or not. Today, there are a plethora of different types of bottles to help with milk intake and digestion, and a good bottle will help to prevent intestinal distress. Oftentimes, it will simply take trying a few different brands to see what works best for your baby's feeding process, as no two babies ever prove to be the same. Glass instead of plastic bottles have recently become an issue of debate for many mothers.

Some mothers feel that the chemicals found in plastic bottles ultimately will be harmful to a baby and should be avoided. Plastic bottles made from polycarbonate that contain the mark PC or are coded with a recycling No. 7 are considered suspect. According to the FDA, using bottles made with the plastic bisphenol A, or BPA, may have an effect on the brain, behavior, and prostate gland in young children. While at this time research on the long-term effects of exposure to BPA is insufficient, the FDA is supporting stricter regulations for BPA oversight.

Another consideration when choosing a bottle should be if you will be supplementing nursing, which is useful if you have difficulty breast-feeding. If this is the case, certain bottles simulate breast-feeding and make the transition between breast and bottle-feeding easier.

After choosing bottles, naturally comes choosing what goes in the bottle: formula or breast milk? Choosing a type of formula is something that is good to discuss with your child's pediatrician. If a newborn has been started on a specific type of formula while at the hospital, it is not a good idea to abruptly change to a different brand. Abruptly switching the type of formula you are feeding you infant can cause gastrointestinal stress and an upset stomach.

A pediatrician who works in the hospital where you are delivering will be able to advise you on what formula the hospital uses so you are able to purchase that brand prior to your birthing experience. Having a ready supply of formula when you bring your baby home is not only wise planning but also proves to be quite convenient.

If you have chosen to breast-feed, it is good to purchase or rent a breast pump prior to the arrival of your baby. Many hospitals offer breast pumps on a lease or rental basis to mothers who have chosen to breast-feed. Breast-feeding is an option that costs nothing aside from the breast pump and bottles, and for many single mothers struggling with a tight budget, this proves advantageous. There are many other benefits afforded to both mother and child when choosing to breast-feed an infant.

The American Academy of Pediatrics recommends breast-feeding for a minimum of six months. Breast-feeding reduces the risk of breast cancer for the mother. There have been studies proving babies who are breast-fed get sick less often, have fewer allergies, and have a stronger immune system during their first months.

Mothers who choose not to breast-feed do so for a variety of reasons. Some mothers do not produce an adequate supply of milk to nourish their infants and so they cannot nurse. Other mothers cannot nurse due to their work schedules or choose to bottle-feed to make it possible for someone other than themselves to feed their baby. When bottle-feeding, a mother can determine the exact amount of formula an infant is receiving, so bottle-feeding can prove advantageous when monitoring an infant's food intake.

While breast-feeding is more convenient, as there is no bottle warming or additional supplies required to feed the baby, it is a personal choice and one that every mother has the right to make. What will work for you and your situation is what you should take into account when making your decision, not necessarily what others before you have chosen to do.

Single Mothers Speak

Scherry Marie Brady, mother of one

"Having a baby on my own has brought me to a place where I am able to juggle multiple tasks. It brought me to a place of being responsible — super responsible — and very organized. I think having a newborn on my own taught me immense understanding and compassion for others going through struggles and difficult times. While it has not always been easy, being a single mother has developed me into a stronger and more capable woman."

Baby-proofing

After you have purchased all the supplies you will need when you bring home your baby, it is time to baby-proof your house. Obviously, an infant will not be able to get into many of the things that you will be baby-proofing. However, being proactive and attending to this when you do not have your baby consuming your time allows you to be more thorough and focused on preparing to keep your baby safe in the future.

First, go around your home and look for anything that is hazardous or poisonous, including medications. Make sure that all cleaning products can be stowed in locked cabinets, and that plants that are poisonous are removed from the home or placed out of reach of a child.

Make a sweep of your home, removing anything that a baby's quick-handed swipe could easily grab or pull. Look at your house from the vantage point of a child. Survey what would be within their reach, and anything that poses a threat must be removed. All outlets need to have outlet covers over them. Cabinets should have locks on them to prevent a child from opening them. Access to water dishes, buckets, or water supplies — such as toilets — should be removed from a child's way. Young children have been known to drown in as much water as a toilet has in a regularly filled bowl.

While these are some basic precautionary moves that can be made prior to the arrival of a new child, there are more exhaustive lists available. Pediatrician's offices often will provide an in-depth outline of how best to prep your house. There are also websites that will provide you with valuable information. The website Keepkideshealthy.com provides a printable list detailing necessary preparation and items for your new arrival at **www.keepkidshealthy.com/newborn/preparing.html**.

The next thing you should do is make a list of emergency contact names and numbers to place by your phone in the event they might be necessary. On this list, include your pediatrician's number and the number of a family member or friend who can come at a moment's notice to drive you to the doctor or an emergency room. It is also a good idea to have the poison control center's number as well as the number of a local taxi service in the event you are not able to drive. You should also find out what emergency room your child's pediatrician is affiliated with. If you are not sure of the directions to this specific hospital, get the directions and keep them with your list of names and numbers.

In preparation to return home after your hospital stay or when you are bringing your baby home for the first time, it is good to have some basic food items on hand so that a trip to the grocery store will not be necessary — these items can include your favorite snacks, quick meals, frozen dinners, and pasta and soup. You may also want to purchase an abundance of feminine products to have one hand if you have delivered your newborn. Purchase these items prior to your baby coming home. You may even want to make some meals and freeze them to use at a later date. Having basic necessities on hand will preclude having to run out to purchase something you desperately need during those first few days or weeks of this huge adjustment. Whether you are carrying a baby, adopting, or bringing a child into the world through a surrogate, these preparations need to be in place.

Having things in place, whether it is groceries or diapers, will make the adjustment to single motherhood a smoother one. Do not be dismayed; with any type of adjustment there are bumpy times and unexpected events, but you and your new baby will survive together.

Every Mother Needs to Adjust

Every mother — not just single mothers — experiences a period of adjustment when she finds herself alone with her child for the first time. It is not abnormal to feel a range of emotions. At times, you may feel that being a single mother will not be as difficult as you had imagined; other times, you may feel so overwhelmed you question your sanity at having taken on such a monumental venture on your own. These are both normal reactions. Every mother, single or not, feels an emotional onslaught with the arrival of a newborn.

It is good for a single mother to connect with someone close to her. You can think of this person as your accountability partner who will be with you during those first few months of transition. Often, when you are in the midst of a depressive state, it is difficult to reach out or know that you need to ask for help. For a single mother, it is important to have a trusted touchstone person in your life. Have them keep tabs on your emotions and be a gauge to alert you if your emotions come to a place of an unhealthy extreme. For example, if you have extreme or violent angry outbursts, or fear of being alone with your baby, these are unhealthy emotional reactions.

Have your accountability partner take note of your actions. If you seem to react in an overly emotional way, for example spells of extreme anger or uncontrollable crying, have him or her address these issues with you. Sleeplessness, beyond that of being awakened by your baby, can also be a sign of an emotional imbalance and should be noted. Also, after you have discussed these issues with your accountability partner, make a plan to take proactive steps to get help. Whether you first consult with your primary care physician or another doctor, it is important to get evaluated by a professional.

All mothers, whether they have given birth, adopted, or used a surrogate, will have a time of emotional adjustment when a newborn is brought home. All mothers of newborns can feel exhilaration and overwhelming joy at holding their new child, but they can just as easily have feelings of anxiety and fear when holding that same little one.

Not just the baby blues

Heightened emotions are normal at this stage. However, if you begin to do things that you know are not rational responses to normal occurrences — wanting to do your baby harm or feeling suicidal or hopeless — it is important for you or the ones closest to you to take note. Other extreme responses or feelings can include having trouble bonding or caring for your baby, extreme mood swings, withdrawal from relationships, or feelings of wanting to harm yourself or your child.

Some mothers experience times of extreme depression following the birth of a child that have been medically classified as postpartum depression, with symptoms and effects varying from woman to woman. Some symptoms of postpartum depression can include sleeplessness, extreme depression, loss of joy in circumstances, noticeable change in weight, fatigue, and loss of concentration. These are just a few of the symptoms; there are many more not listed here.

Mothers Know Best

Florence McGarrity, family counselor

"Postpartum depression has nothing to do with whether you love your baby or not, it has nothing to do with your desire to be a mother. Postpartum depression is a condition that many mothers, regardless of their circumstances, suffer from. Even those mothers who have adopted a baby have been known to suffer emotionally at this juncture in their mothering. Too frequently, people have discounted the emotions associated with postpartum depression and allowed them to go untreated or largely ignored. Choosing to ignore this condition is harmful to both mother and child."

Postpartum depression is treatable, and this condition should not go untreated because it can cause lasting harm to both mother and child. The Mayo Clinic, which can be accessed online at **www.mayoclinic.com**, offers detailed information including postpartum depression symptoms to treatment options.

Should you experience any of these symptoms or similar ones, it is important to speak with someone. It would be wise to consult a professional, for example your ob/gyn or pediatrician, who is adept at assessing these types of situations. Should they determine that you need help or medical intervention, it is better to have addressed the situation at the earliest onset rather than to risk an unhealthy situation for you or your baby.

Sleep deprivation, which is common during the beginning of motherhood, is also a cause of heightened emotionality. Newborns sleep in patterns that may vary from night to night. With very little sleep, mothers tend to feel less able to handle the day-to-day occurrences in their lives. This sleep deprivation cycle is normal, and it is not exclusive to single mothers; partnered mothers experience this as well. All mothers will need to adjust when a newborn's sleep schedule causes disruptions for her regular sleeping pattern. Though it might feel like you are alone in this experience because you are the only one waking up each night to care for the baby, you are not alone in your experience; all new mothers are subject this pattern of sleep deprivation.

This adjustment phase is normal and nothing you should panic about. However, as questions arise, do not hesitate to consult your pediatrician or trusted friends who are mothers and most assuredly experienced similar situations. While advice can prove to be invaluable, trust that you have a certain wisdom you are beginning to acquire while taking care of your child. You will learn your child's wants and needs in a way no other person can; you will be sensitive and in tune with the signals he or she is giving you. Eventually, you will learn your child's cries and his or her behavior patterns.

Now that your role has gone from expectant mother to single mother, take a moment to enjoy all that is around you. Hold yourself still long enough to hear your little one breathe. Take pleasure in watching your infant learn and grow. Enjoy these moments, as they will go very quickly. And, just as you are turning the pages of this book to the next chapter, you will be turning to the next chapter in the life of your child.

Chapter 4

Adjustment for All —Settling into Single Motherhood

The first step in adjusting to single motherhood is to sit down and take a deep breath. Give yourself the freedom to acknowledge you are incapable of being a "perfect mother;" no one is perfect, and everyone is bound to make mistakes. But, as daunting as it may seem at times, you and your child will survive. Next, make sure you are able to laugh. Laughter during all this change and at times of upheaval in your life will make it bearable and will promote healthy living and healing. If you need help finding something humorous, try renting some slapstick comedies or, if you have the money to do so, visit a local comedy club. Either option can provide a respite from life's realities and give you a good dose of belly laughter.

> *"Just because everything is different doesn't mean anything has changed."*
>
> — *Irene Peter*
> *American writer*

With these two survival techniques fixed in your mind — allowing yourself to breathe and making sure you laugh — it is time to acknowledge that change is on its way. Change is inevitably unsettling, no matter if it is thrust upon you or if you choose it. As a single mom, the way you navigate the changes in life will largely be the barometer for how your children navigate their new circumstances. How single mothers react to the transition into motherhood will largely affect the attitude their children bring to their experience.

You are not a thermometer in your child's life; you are a thermostat — you set the temperature for how your child acclimates to his or her new lifestyle and family dynamic. In adjusting to the new needs of life, it is important to determine what truly is the best situation you and your child. There are many options that are now available for the single mother, and these should be exhaustively explored. These options include, but are not limited to, programs designed specifically for the benefit of single mothers, co-ops, shared housing, work or job programs, and many other options to research and take full advantage of. These options are designed and tailored to specifically address a single mother's issues and can aid in a wide range of needs. Often, these programs can facilitate getting temporary financial aid, locating housing, and even offering child care solutions.

Regardless of how you came to embark on the road of single motherhood, there is one undeniable fact: Life will change. It seems a simple statement, and one that might not need to be addressed. However, there are many mothers who go into parenting on their own believing very little in their life and in their routine will change. Accept that there will be changes and that what works one day will not necessarily work the next. How you choose to view these changes — and adapt to them — will largely determine the tone for your life and that of your children. If you constantly say how bad things are and how sad you are, this will translate into an attitude that your little ones will feel, no matter how small they are.

It is important to take note of the positives in your situation. If you need to, make a list — every day if you have to — of those things that are good in your life and the lives of your children. Remind your children and yourself of these positive things in your life. Enumerate them. The glass can either be half full or half empty; how you interpret your circumstances is entirely in your control.

Single Mothers Speak
Tracy Faith, *mother of one*

"Admittedly, being a single mother is not always easy. And, I did not become a single mother by choice. However, being a single mother has made me a better and stronger woman. I have learned to fight for what I want."

While the circumstances of you becoming a single mother may not have been ideal, you are not a victim. If you have let yourself think of yourself as a victim of circumstance, from this point on, change your thinking process and instead choose to take control and to be in control. You define how you interpret your circumstances, so make a choice to live in a place of forward thinking. You will be far more able to cope with challenges that arise in a healthy and beneficial way if you are not conceding defeat before you even begin to tackle these obstacles.

Times Are Changing

The times have changed and single mothers are no longer a paltry minority. Statistics show there are more than 21.7 million children under the age of 21 who are being raised in a single-parent household. As of 2003, 43.7 percent of mothers who had custody of their children were either separated or divorced. When you enroll your child in school, he or she will no longer be the only child who comes from a single-parent family. The father, mother, and child structure is not generally the way it is any longer. Now, children often split time between two households, and there are even single fathers handling all the parenting duties. Knowing this should make it easier for single moms to navigate their new lifestyle.

Strategies for Adjusting
Get proper rest

Each of us has a different time clock, which means each of us requires different amounts of sleep to function at our peak performance level. Lack of sleep is torture; in fact, sleep deprivation is a technique used to weaken and debilitate people. When we are deprived of proper rest, we become more emotional and less capable of handling normal daily routines. Rest is imperative for a single mom.

If you have a newborn or young child, try to sleep when he or she is napping. Follow their sleep patterns so you are not staying up for hours when they are resting. To aid in the goal of getting more rest, understand that not everything will always get done by the end of the day and that is all right. Deciding between doing an extra load of laundry and getting an extra hour of sleep should not be a tough decision; take a nap — the time to sleep will not always be available, but the time to do laundry will.

Get involved

One of the quickest ways to become comfortable in any situation is to get involved. Volunteer to help out at school or with an activity your child participates in; this will give you the opportunity to meet other parents. Volunteering in a school or program your child is involved with gives you a better feeling about yourself. You are contributing, and there is nothing better for our psyches than to give something back.

First Step to Adjusting – For Your Children

Keep in mind that just as you need time to adjust to the changes in your life, your child needs the same opportunity. The grief they are experiencing, while different than your own, is no less painful or consequential; it is simply different. The first thing to keep in mind for your children when settling them into a new life is that children are creatures of habit. They are most comfortable when there is a distinct pattern in their lives, and they thrive on order.

The first step to keep your children balanced — and to make life easier for all concerned — is to create a schedule. When first implementing a schedule, as a mother you may face some opposition. However, consistently stick with it and your children will soon adapt. To get your child or children used to a routine, schedule bedtime beginning with a predictable evening routine, which will help avoid arguments when bedtime occurs. Next, consider each day of the week and what activities occur on each day for you and your children. Map out where you need to be and when. Include family time and chores within the scheduling.

The more organized you are, the less overwhelmed and fatigued you will tend be. Many mothers feel that it is advantageous to post a schedule in a family room or kitchen so that all the family members are aware of what is happening when.

The following are some suggestions that may prove helpful when creating a daily schedule for you and your children:

- Begin by analyzing your daily events. Take note of times when conflicts may arise so that you will be able to later address them by adjusting your schedule.

- Determine the goals for your schedule. Do you need more time in the morning for everyone to eat and get on their way on time? Or, do you want a more organized evening so that homework gets done first thing rather than last thing at night?

- Write everything down. Make lists of each person's daily routine and activities.

- Create a schedule.

- Place the schedule in a part of the house that your family members use regularly.

- Follow the schedule for at least a week before making any changes or adjustments to it.

If your children are older, let them help create this new plan of events. Allow them to voice their concerns, and also allow them the opportunity to suggest ways of doing things that would make it easier for them to adapt to their new circumstances. Remember, they are also adjusting in ways that are scary and at times uncomfortable. When you allow your child or children to have a voice, it makes them feel more in control of the events that seem to control their lives. Allow this new schedule to be one that will simplify your life as a mother instead of complicate it.

Family Schedule for Wednesday

	Mother	David	Tracy	Benji
6-7 a.m.	get up	get up	get up	
7-8 a.m.	get ready	get ready	get ready	get up
8-9 a.m.	breakfast	Breakfast-bus	Breakfast-bus	Breakfast-day care
9-10 a.m.	work	school	school	day care
10-11 a.m.	work	school	school	day care
11-12 p.m.	work	school	school	day care
12-1 p.m.	work	school	school	day care
1-2 p.m.	work	school	school	day care
2-3 p.m.	work	school	school	day care
3-4 p.m.	work	school	school	day care
4-5 p.m.	Work-pick up	football	cheerleading	pick up from day care
5-6 p.m.	home	football	cheerleading	playtime
6-7 p.m.	home	football	cheerleading	playtime
7-8 p.m.	pick up	pick up	pick up	playtime
8-9 p.m.	dinner	dinner	dinner	dinner
9-10 p.m.	clean up	homework	homework	bed
10-11p.m.	bed	bed	bed	

Another suggestion is to grant each child a voice in the decision-making process; this will help them feel that while things in their lives are in a state of change, they are still permitted to have some semblance of control. For younger children, you can allow them to choose if they take a bath before or after dinner — if this is feasible with the timing of dinner. Or you can allow them to choose if they want dessert before or after their bath time. Small decisions allow children to feel they have a sense of control, even when their world is drastically changing.

Ask older children about their feelings regarding scheduling their time or when choosing activities. If you must omit an activity because of budgetary reasons, do not make the choice for your child; instead allow him or her to be a part of the decision-making process by having a say in what he or she would like to do. However, only ask for their opinion or for their input when you can accommodate their preferences. It will frustrate a child when you ask for his or her opinion and then ignore it completely. For example, if because of budgetary reasons you have to reduce the activities your child is participating in, ask him or her which one he or she would most like to continue. If there is no cost differentiation, allow his or her decision to stand.

In your attempt to help your children adjust, it is often helpful to inform their teachers of the changes they are experiencing so the school system can be not only accommodating but also more understanding. Teachers should be advised to not share this information but simply to take it into consideration when a child is more sensitive or is acting out in a manner uncharacteristic to him or her. Sharing this information is not intended to put your child under the scrutiny of a spotlight but to instead help him or her adjust to new circumstances.

Anticipation is another great way to take the focus off a new situation that may be uncomfortable for your child. Make plans to do something together that you know your child will really enjoy. Tell your child about your plans so they will grow excited about them. Oftentimes, removing your child from his or her day-to-day routine is helpful. For example, you and your child can take a nature walk in a national park that is some distance from your home or go to the beach and play catch or football.

If you are a single mother of older children or teenagers, it is often a good idea to consult them when planning an outing. Ask them what they would like to do. Have them make a list so there are more options for you to consider. If an older child does not want to participate in an activity primarily geared to a younger child, schedule time for just you and him or her at a later date. Consider doing something with the older child that you would not include the younger children in. Often, for example, there are movies that are not appropriate for your younger child but entirely appropriate for a more mature child. Set aside a time when you can take your older child to a movie that he or she would enjoy. This not only will give you the opportunity for some one-on-one time, which is important, but it will also make your older child feel that his or her needs are taken into consideration. Going to a museum or lunch and browsing through a bookstore with a teen girl or a sporting event, a hike, or an art gallery visit with a teenage boy are also a few suggestions.

Though children often prove more resilient than we realize, it is important to keep a close watch on your child as they are adjusting to their new environment. If they begin to act out in ways that are detrimental to themselves or others, it is important to address this immediately. If your child exhibits erratic behavior, displays dramatic changes in his or her appearance or habits, loses or gains a significant amount of weight, or exhibits any other out of character changes, it is important to take note and be proactive. Do not wait to seek help for your child; the sooner a problem is addressed, the fewer consequences there will be.

For some single mothers, adjusting to your new lifestyle will require you to send your child to day care or after-school care. Your presentation of this change will largely influence how he or she interprets the situation. If you need to cry about leaving them at a facility for care, save your tears until you are out of sight of your child. If a child senses you are upset, they will take his or her cues from you and become upset themselves.

Choosing Child Care

Finding child care for your new baby or for a not yet school-aged little one can seem at first like a daunting task. However, with a bit if ingenuity and research, it does not have to be.

There are some easily accessible resources to help you begin your search. A look at the phone book will provide an initial list of child care locations. Consulting with the local school system can offer insight, as well. Oftentimes, local schools will partner with child care providers to offer after school care for older children, as well as care for children who are not old enough to attend school. With this in mind, it may be helpful to choose a child care provider where your child would be able to continue attending even after he or she is in school. Whatever you choose for your child, a local school can prove to be a good resource for information.

Single Mothers Speak

Scherry Marie Brady, mother of one

"I found that there were a lot of services and options for child care. The thing was I really had to be the one to pursue them. The first place I had my daughter, when she was an infant, was a licensed day care provider out of a private home. This worked well because she got a lot of one-on-one attention. At age 3, when I went to college, she attended the college's day care program. She went to this program until she was 5 and began attending school. Once she was enrolled in kindergarten, she went to school in the daytime and after school she was bussed to the local Head Start program, which ended at 6 p.m. In the evening, I picked her up after I finished work. This worked well for us, but each time she switched places, it took me a lot of leg work to find the right place."

Another resource for finding child care is using the Internet. One popular website to visit is Care.com (**www.care.com**). Not only will you be able to search the websites of day care centers, but you can also access the Better Business Bureau for your area and check to see if any of the day care centers you are looking into have had complaints filed against them.

There are many types of child care with different settings and offerings. There is in-home child care, private day care, institutional day care, babysitting, and work-sponsored day care. There are numerous options available to suit your needs as a single mother with children of any age. The first step in choosing child care is to determine your needs. Some questions you should ask yourself when considering child care options include:

- How many hours do you work outside of the home?

- Would your job be willing to accommodate you working remotely for some part of the week?

- Does your employer offer child care?

- How much are you able to spend on child care?

Once you answer these questions, you can develop a plan to address your specific child care needs. If you are pregnant, do not wait until after you give birth to find a child care provider for your newborn. Oftentimes, there are waiting lists for programs and evaluations that have to conducted before your child can be accepted into program.

Asking family members

Family members are a good resource for child care, provided they are willing and able to assist you. Family can also be a supplemental provider; for example, having your child stay with a family member two days a week and in a day care program the other three can help defray the costs of child care, as it can drain a single parent's budget. When considering placing your child in the care of a family member, it is important to establish boundaries prior to enlisting the person's help. Clearly define the days and hours that you would need a family member to care for your child, and also define whether the family member will be paid. Do not wait to answer these questions; discuss the questions and his or her answers prior to ever enlisting the help. This will allow for healthier and friendlier relationships between family members.

Finding in-home child care

Akin to a family member offering child care is the option of in-home child care. Au pairs, nannies, and baby sitters offer the ease of having child care in your home. However, this can be an expensive child care option. Oftentimes, mothers will choose to have their caregiver live with them for further convenience. Should you decided to hire an au pair or nanny, it is important to go through an agency or do extensive screening — background check, drug screening, etc. — for anyone who will be caring for your child along with having free access to your home. Most staffing agencies provide complete background checks on the nannies or au pairs they hire. This is one of the benefits of going through an agency instead of placing an advertisement for a care provider in a newspaper or online.

Agencies are listed in the phone book or can be found by going to the Nanny Authority website found at **www.nannyauthority.com** or the International Nanny Association's website at **www.nanny.org**. These websites provide a look into the specific agencies and the screening process that the nannies they represent must undergo prior to being placed within a home. As well, they offer guidance in choosing the right nanny for your children and your unique situation. This will help ensure the nanny you choose will meet your specific needs. Also, the site will help you understand what you can expect from a nanny, the services they will provide, and what a nanny will expect of you, from salary guidelines to housing and cooking arrangements.

When choosing an au pair or a nanny, it is important for you to feel safe and secure with the type of care the person will provide. Simply because you choose to go through an agency does not ensure you will be pleased with the person or people they refer to you. Take your time. Do not feel embarrassed to ask extensive questions and to spend time with the person before making a final decision whether to hire him or her to care for your child.

At-home day care

Similar to in-home child care is the at-home care option. As opposed to a franchised or privately owned day care center, there are people who offer day care or child care services out of their home. This option is often less costly than a franchised or privately owned day care center, and it offers that homey environment instead of a more institutional one. However, there are some things to consider before choosing this type of child care. First, check to see if the day care provider has the licenses your state requires. Per your request, a child care provider must show you their state-certified license. You should also request visits not only with the provider but at a time the children in his or her care are present. Should you get to the point of seriously considering the provider, it is often a good idea to bring your child for a visit before fully committing yourself to this person's services. It is reassuring to see how your child interacts with a child care provider prior to the first time he or she is left in the provider's care.

Larger day care facilities

A franchised, privately owned, or non-profit day care facility usually can accommodate a greater number of children than in-home options. These facilities tend to be more structured and have defined hours of operations with very little leeway in these times. The staff of these operations usually have undergone training before they are able to care for children. For example, they may be required to be certified in infant and child CPR prior to being permitted to supervise children. Make sure you clearly understand the payment and fee policies. If you are often late leaving work, see if there is a fee incurred for a late pick-up. Also, check to see what the policy is for holidays, as some places are not open on holidays when you may have to work. There are often waiting lists with these facilities, so it is best to check into them as soon as you realize that you will need child care. If you are currently pregnant or an adoptive mother who will soon be expecting, do not put off researching child care options until you have brought your child home with you. Be proactive; the last thing you will feel the desire to do with a new little one in your arms is trek to a child care facility.

Child care options at work

As more mothers are returning to work, some companies have started offering in-building child care, which means a child care center is staffed and run within the company's building. This child care opportunity can be very advantageous for the working single mother, as it provides great convenience and hours of operation are concurrent with your company's work demands. Should your child get sick or need you for any reason, you are available. While this option is becoming more prevalent, it is still not offered by all large companies.

Regardless of the child care center you choose, all child care facilities should have an open-door policy, meaning at any time, you should be able to stop by and visit your child. This helps ensure there is nothing hidden going on. Also, make a point of checking with the local Better Business Bureau to see if any complaints have been filed against the child care provider in the past. You are entitled to this information because it is public record; do not hesitate to request it.

As with finding a pediatrician, a mother's greatest resource for assistance in finding a child care provider will be other mothers and their references. Mothers whose children attend specific programs are able to give more insight into the realities of a child care program. Referrals from one parent to another are invaluable. Also, if there is a lengthy waiting list, sometimes knowing someone whose child currently attends your center of choice can help speed up the process.

Work Schedule Options

Along with seeking out the best possible child care options, another possibility is amending your work schedule to better suit your child's schedule. Many companies now have the potential for working remotely. While you may not be able to do this five days a week, working remotely a day or two a week oftentimes is an option.

Single Mothers Speak
Tara Surowiec, mother of two

"Before I adopted my daughter, I checked out all my scheduling options with my employer. I was candid with them about what I was considering and what that would mean to my work situation. My employer worked with me so that I could be as present as possible for my daughter. I never would have known the options available to me had I not had the courage to approach my employer."

The best way to approach your boss is to have a thought-out plan for how you could do the same amount of work while working from home. When presenting your idea, offer it up as a temporary and conditional arrangement. A trial basis is a good starting point for both you and your employer. Ask for a specific trail period and then request the two of you sit down to evaluate the new working conditions.

As a single mother, one of the mantras that is invaluable to fixate on is "It cannot hurt to ask." This is not just a concept for the work place; it is a very handy approach for solving a great deal of life's single mother dilemmas. You will never know if the day care has a busing service — a service that will bring school-age children to and from the child care location when the school day is concluded — unless you ask. You will never know what your company's policy is on bringing your children to work once a week for a few hours until you ask about it. The only way you will learn about opportunities that will help you and your child is by asking.

Considering Career Changes

Oftentimes, single mothers find that subtle career adjustments or even radical career changes can best suit their new lifestyle. While these choices can take some time to implement, they are worth considering if you find your current work situation, hours, or demands do not work well with raising a child on your own.

If you decide to switch jobs or adjust the hours that you work, the first place to begin your search for creating your ideal job situation is with your current employer. Your current employer may be able to adjust to you working a few days a week from home or creating four longer work days, allowing you to have an additional day off per week. While your current employer may not be able to adjust to a remote work situation or allow for a flexible time schedule, there may be other employers that do. You need to investigate these options before making any decisions or job changes. When you find a company that has a position you are interested in, the first step in the investigative process would be calling the human resources department.

Human resource departments can provide invaluable information on the work atmosphere and policies of their particular company. Hiring procedures, with an explanation of the company's protocol for receiving a list of available positions or setting up an interview, can be requested. A human resource department can also provide guidelines on telecommuting and the company's work-from-home policy. This department would also be able to provide you with information on whether the company provides any type of on-site or work-related child care.

Keep in mind you do not want to make a job or career change without an assured job lined up. As a single mother, you have to proactively plan for you and your child. In today's economy, it is unwise to leave a job without another job already in place.

Another possibility to investigate is starting a home-based business if your career choice allows you to do this. A home-based business can allow a single mother the ability to be available for her child. Also, while considering a home-based business, another possibility is to see if your interests could have the potential for making money. For example, if you enjoy baking, could you create enough business by supplying local restaurants with pies, cakes, and desserts? Or, would your interest and enjoyment in planning family parties lead you to an event planning business? These are just two suggestions to help you begin to think of other opportunities. Do not overlook your unique potential. Begin with your unique strengths and go from there. Even your expertise as a mom and running a household on your own should not be overlooked. The key to success is using skills you already have well honed.

Consider the stories of these two self-starters. Do the names Julie Aigner-Clark or Doris Christopher mean anything to you? Julie Aigner-Clark left her job when she became a mother. Aigner-Clark wanted a challenging job she could orchestrate from home, so she began making educationally entertaining videos and learning devices. She started what is now known as Baby Einstein. Doris Christopher wanted to have the opportunity to be a stay at home mom but also wanted an income. She used her background as a former home economics teacher to create the line of kitchen gadgets sold from women's homes across the country and now known as The Pampered Chef.

Becoming Your Own Boss

Another option for single moms is to be your own boss. One of the ways to do this without really having to entirely go out on your own is to open a franchise. Although opening a franchise can prove to be costly, it is not as risky for a single mother because you are under the umbrella of a larger company. According to the Small Business Association, women partially own 30 percent of franchises and wholly own 10 percent of all franchises in the United States. In attempt to encourage more female business owners, there is a support organization called the Women's Franchise Committee that holds an annual meeting distinctly for the purpose of supporting female franchise owners. The venue specifically targets networking opportunities for attendees as well as expansion possibilities. For more information on the conference, go to **www.franchise.org/FranchiseeSecondary.aspx?id=22132**. The organization also has local chapters designed specifically for women where they can share ideas, exchange information, and support one another as business owners.

Pursuing Further Education

When considering a career change for a position outside of your current industry, one way to begin preparing is by taking classes in your field of interest, which would add time to your schedule. However, with a long-term goal in mind, a single mother can be motivated to acquire further education to have the life she desires for her and her child or children.

Single Mothers Speak
Kieran Ross, mother of two

"I am working full time as a paraprofessional in a special education class. I am also going to school full time. I take classes online, so I am able to be at home with my children and still work toward my degree without ever having to leave the house. Going to school and earning my teaching degree will afford me and my children a better future. Having my teaching certificate will greatly increase my earning potential."

If you are looking for a new job within your industry, taking classes within your career track can also allow more flexibility in your current work situation. The more education you have in your field, the more you have to offer your employer, which could mean the more willing your employer will be to accommodate changes in your work schedule or environment. The more educated you are, the greater your earning potential.

Thanks to technology, there are numerous online classes and seminars that provide opportunities for furthering your education in your career path. These allow you to study and attend classes at your convenience in your home. When checking into online classes and programs, it is important to take note of the accreditation of the program. Any program issuing diplomas or certifications is required by law to state if and where they receive accreditation. A fully accredited program will allow you to transfer the credits you acquire to any college degree program. However, there are a number of programs that are not accredited and do not count toward a degree program; these are often not accepted by employers as valid. For a complete explanation of how and why accredited programs are important, go to the Back to College website at **www.back2college.com/library/accreditfaq.htm**.

Another option for establishing academic credits and finishing an undergraduate degree is an adult degree completion program. Many traditional college programs, along with their four-year degrees, are now offering a one-year program to complete an undergraduate degree. These are intense programs that combine life experience credits, which are determined by the academic institution and apply to your degree, with academic credits. Check with the institution you are considering to see if they permit life experience credits and what their policy is regarding obtaining them.

Nyack College, located in Nyack, New York, is one example of a traditional four-year college that also offers the non-traditional approach of an adult degree completion program. This program allows students to complete a bachelor of science degree in organizational leadership in 14 months. Students are permitted to apply for credits through life experiences, whether in prior work-acquired skills or through life circumstances.

Adult degree completion programs are structured so those attending are able to attend school while continuing to work. Most programs are set up so those participating need to only go to class one day a week for a four- or five-hour class. Listings online are available for programs of this type, and local colleges can also provide directions as to the most convenient programs they offer. For those who do not have an undergraduate degree, these programs can provide a manageable time commitment for a single mother. One evening or afternoon a week for a year is much easier to fit within a schedule than four years of ongoing classes.

Continuing or furthering your education will put you in a place of developing connections and networking, thus creating greater opportunities for possible future employment opportunities. Some companies provide compensation for employees who are furthering their education and attending an accredited program.

While all these suggestions for gaining further education sound grand, the big question often looming before a single mother becomes how will you fit classes into your schedule and how will you afford to pay for school? As a single mother, time is a valuable commodity. Going to school will require adjustments to your and your child's schedule. However, going back to school can be done class by class over a longer period of time or in an intensive program. While time constraints may loom, strategic scheduling — whether it is for your work schedule for your child's schedule — can make it possible for a single mother to earn a coveted degree. It may take longer and require compromise on everyone's part, but it is not an impossible goal to achieve.

Once you have determined that you will attend school and have selected a program you are interested in, make an appointment with a financial aid advisor. This appointment is free, and you will be under no obligation to attend school there or take on loans. A financial aid advisor will provide you with the forms you are required to complete for eligibility for financial assistance when attending the school of your choice. Once these forms have been completed, they will generate a statement of eligibility that outlines what type of assistance you are eligible for. However, if you do not receive loans and grants from the school of your choice, do not give up on the idea of going to that particular school until you have done further research. There are numerous grants and scholarships available to single mothers, and there are numerous opportunities that go untapped each year. Scholarship searches are simple to initiate, especially with the help of online resources. The most direct and easily accessible site is Scholarships.com (**www.scholarships.com**). This site offers free scholarship searches, application strategies, and financial aid information and tips. The College Board website also offers a comprehensive search vehicle on their site, **www.collegeboard.com**.

Some scholarship search programs charge a fee for their services, and these services tend to be more exhaustive. With a beginning rate of $25, fees range from service to service and depend upon how exhaustive they are. Some services have prices that range up to a few hundred dollars. However, some charge no fee but simply have you fill out forms online and produce results for those scholarships that you might possibly qualify for. If you have the time, you may be able to find a scholarship you qualify for simply by doing extensive research on your own. This is a time-consuming process, but it is worth the time, as it will save you the potential of large amount of loans to repay.

Grants and scholarships can range anywhere from a few hundred dollars to the amount of an entire semester, including cost of books. Finding grants and scholarships can necessitate some initial work and research but will prove worthwhile, as it will reduce the debt a single mother will incur while furthering her education. The monetary amount for grants and scholarships differ from program to program and from institution to institution.

While considering returning to school and all the other life-style changes you are facing in your adjustment to single motherhood, it is important to remember that throughout this process you have to continue to take care of yourself. Part of taking care of yourself and taking care for your children is establishing a healthy relationship with their father. This is imperative for all involved, but most especially for your children. While you may no longer be co-parenting in the same home or you may never have co-parented, you need to learn that operating as a team is the best option you can offer your children.

Chapter 5

The Other Half — My Child's Father

According to the most recent data released by the U.S. Census Bureau, there are approximately 54.5 million married couples raising children and approximately 12.9 million single women raising children. It is reported that the most common way a woman becomes a single mother is through divorce. Roughly 15

> *"When one door of happiness closes, another opens; but often we look so long at the closed door that we do not see the one which has been opened for us."*
>
> *– Helen Keller*
> *American author and political activist*
> *June 27, 1880 – June 1, 1968*

million children have experienced a divorce. Considering these findings, it is quite possible you found your way to single motherhood by the dissolution of your marriage. While this statistic may seem staggering, it should also encourage you to know that there are others who are also making their way through the aftermath of divorce and subsequently raising children on their own. You are not alone in what you are facing.

For your children, divorce is a crisis in their lives, and as a mother, your deepest desire is to prevent your child from hurting or feeling the pain of something that is not their choice or their doing. You want to keep them from pain, and you want to have them feel no consequences of the divorce.

Unfortunately, there is no perfect way to steer your children through the maze of divorce and guarantee that they will remain unscathed. As a single mother, you must allow yourself to understand that you can only do so much. However, do not forsake helping your children because you acknowledge the bumps in the road are inevitable and that there will be tough times ahead. As a mother, you are in a unique position to provide support and guidance through this entire process. You will set the tone for how well your children adapt to the divorce or the absence of their father in their lives.

There are a few basic ways that a mother can foster an environment that will facilitate a much healthier and positive adjustment. First, create a stable home life for your children. What this means is to create a lifestyle that is routine. At first, try to keep as much of the routine that existed prior to the divorce as possible. This is especially important early on, as many things will be rapidly changing during the first few months of the divorce. Letting children know that dinner will be served at a consistent time, what their chores are, what time curfew is, and that the new schedule you create will be adhered to are all ways of creating a stable environment. Another basic way is to create consistent opportunities for open communication. Children need to feel that they can come to you with any and all concerns that they may have.

One way to do this is to consistently ask your children questions about what is happening in their lives. While you may often get a one-word response, continue showing your children that you are interested in what is important to them. Another way to create opportunities for communication, especially in households with more than one child, is to set aside a specific time to spend alone with each child to foster an environment of intimacy. For example, you can take your daughter to lunch once a month. Make a commitment to yourself that you will not discuss anything but positive things that she is doing while you are enjoying lunch. Do not use this time to discuss a recent punishment or a problem you are having with her, unless she specifically addresses the issue. Time set aside for communication, no matter the venue, is important for children. The more that you as a mother create opportunities for your child to talk to you, the more likely he or she will be to talk and share his or her feelings.

Regardless of your child's age, it is important for him or her to come to an understanding that the divorce had nothing to do with him or her. Children need to understand that the divorce is in no way their fault, and they could not have done anything to prevent it. Make it clear to your children this decision was made between you and their father. Providing this kind of reassurance needs to be done on an ongoing basis as all of you settle into a new routine and new circumstances.

Mothers Know Best

Florence McGarrity, family counselor, mother of one, grandmother of one

"One of the best things a mother can do to reassure her child that he or she is not the cause of his or her parents' divorce is to tell the child. Constantly repeat that the child is not the reason that you and your child's father are not together. Tell your child that you and his or her father's feelings have not changed. Your child needs to hear that your love for him or her has not changed. This is a process and takes time, and most children need the reinforcement of repetition."

Older children tend to be much more aware of the events that lead up to the divorce. However, younger children may have been completely unaware that tension existed between you and your former spouse or partner, so this event of separation may come as a shock to them. Keep in mind, a young child's concept of space, time, and events is very different from an older child's or an adult's.

While you are creating a separate life apart from their father, give children as much age-appropriate information as possible. The website KidsGrowth.com can help you better understand your child's age and what is appropriate at each stage of development (**www.kidsgrowth.com/stages/guide/index.cfm**). If you understand what characteristics, attributes, and actions are common in children of a certain age, as a mother, you can more adequately meet your child's age specific needs. Each child is different, and some develop more quickly while others may progress a bit more slowly; however, these general guidelines can prove to be of help.

The fewer surprises children of divorce incur, the more they will begin to relax and to feel safe and secure in their new environment. Surprises can include changes in a child's schedule. Not seeing certain people — friends or your former husband's or boyfriend's family — as often as he or she used to can be another surprise to a child who does not have the ability to deduce that this can occur after a divorce or separation. Or, changes in routine habits can be a surprise to a child. For example, if you always attended services at a specific house of worship and suddenly change this practice because it is uncomfortable to encounter your former spouse, your child may not be able to grasp the reasoning for this. Instead, he or she simply notices that something familiar has disappeared from his or her life. Another example might be the established pattern of going out to dinner as a family on Saturday nights, something that you did prior to your divorce but have not continued. These changes can be disconcerting to a child who is used to a specific routine. As an adult, you have a good sense of reasoning. You know that because you and your child's father are no longer together, there will be changes in your lifestyle while a child does not necessarily have this developed sense of logical reasoning.

When your child — regardless of his or her age — begins to ask questions or wants to talk about his or her issues and concerns, the most important thing you must remember to do is listen. Listen to what he or she is really saying before you even begin to assess what his or her needs are or give answers to the issues he or she is raising. Listen to your child's concerns as well as his or her point of view and questions.

Learning to really hear what your children are saying takes time, patience, and practice. First, really allow your children to tell you things. This means let them talk and finish their sentences; do not immediately offer solutions. Just hear the problem. When a child feels really heard, he or she will be able to move on to begin to solve the problem more quickly than if he or she feels that they are caught up in trying to explain themselves. Oftentimes, a child's problem looms larger because he or she simply feels he or she is the only one shouldering the worry. When you can hear what your child is saying, he or she feels much safer and less alone. A good way to let a child know that you have heard what he or she has said is to repeat to him or her what was just told to you. Begin by saying, "So, what I understand that you are saying is…" If he or she feels that you heard the concerns correctly, he or she will tell you. If what you have said is wrong, give your child the opportunity to correct you. Then restate what he or she has said until you have it right.

While you are listening, remember that the way children see their father may be entirely different than the way that you view him. Keep in mind that just because their viewpoint is not the same as yours does not make either one wrong. Remember they have any entirely unique relationship with their father than you ever will, and vice versa. Your children's feelings are entirely separate from your feelings in regard to their father, and it is important you keep these feelings separated. For the sake of your children and their well-being, keep the dialogue about their father a safe and open topic. Do not criticize them when they say something positive about their father. Allow them the opportunity to express how very much they may miss him, because while you may not miss having your children's father around, your children will feel a void because of his absence. When your children express their feelings, never make them feel that their emotions are wrong or something that they should be ashamed of.

Do not feel guilty about their feelings of missing their father and wanting him back, even if these feelings in no way mirror your own. A child who misses his or her father is in no way reflecting that his or her mother is not doing or being enough as a parent. One way to help yourself relate to your child is by allowing yourself to recall a time when you missed someone dear to you. Then, translate this feeling into an understanding of where your child is. Consider the pain they are experiencing. While it is difficult, try to separate yourself from being an "ex" and focus on being a mother and meeting your child's needs. Allow mothering to take control.

Because children may have feelings of guilt when their parents are divorcing, they may assume they can facilitate bringing you and their father back together. Children may choose to create scenarios in an attempt to bring their parents back together. Whether it is saying they are sick or causing problems at school, oftentimes, children will draw attention to themselves in an attempt to draw their parents together. If you suspect that your child is intentionally orchestrating these circumstances, ask him or her if he or she would like for you and his or her father to be together again. Allow your child the opportunity to share his or her feelings on this subject with you. Then, after he or she has truly shared his or her heart, with tact and gentleness let your child know that you and his or her father have made a decision that is best for all of you and that it will not be changing. If you have a good relationship with your child's father, you may want him to be a part of this conversation. Allow your child to ask any questions he or she may want to ask, and then address each issue with gentleness. Keep in mind your child may feel hurt and disappointed that he or she cannot change the relationship between you and his or her father. Before closing the subject, reiterate that this in no way changes your love for your child.

Some children can aptly voice their feelings and their fears in regard to their parents no longer being married, while other children act out or become depressed or even angry. Children are often afraid that if one parent has left, it may simply be just a matter of time before the other parent leaves too. As well, children can be afraid that they are no longer loved in the same way. Children of divorce may fear that because you are no longer with their father, your feelings for them may have changed too. Reassure your children that they are always loved, whether you and their father are together or not. Whatever their feelings are, do not tell your children not to feel the way they do. Children have a right to their feelings, even if we as adults cannot relate to or understand them.

Psychologists and family therapists advise allowing your child the opportunity to voice their feelings in a constructive manner. This means that children cannot use bad language or yell or scream, and you should instead encourage your children to share how they are feeling. If they do reach a place of being overly emotional, you can tell them, "Maybe you need to take some time to calm down and we can talk about this later. I know that this is very upsetting to you, but we have to treat each other with love and respect, and we cannot continue this conversation until you have calmed down."

If a child is consistently disturbed and overly emotional about the divorce, it is often a good idea to seek out a counselor, therapist, or psychologist to help lead the child through the emotions he or she is experiencing. Choosing to do this before problems develop often proves more effective than waiting until the child begins to exhibit behavioral problems in other areas of his or her life. For example, a boy instigating fights at school because he is frustrated by the circumstances at home or a girl failing to do school work because she is too upset are problems that can result when children act out of frustration. If these issues are proactively addressed verses reactively addressed, the issues tend to be more easily overcome.

Forgive and Forget

The best thing that you can do for your children is to forgive their father of whatever wrong doings you feel he is guilty of. Once you have let go of your anger and any feelings of resentment, you may hold against your former spouse, you will be able to relate to him in a more positive manner.

This in no way is saying that you should condone his bad actions; instead, simply forgive him. When you forgive another person, it may seem that you are letting him or her off the hook. But, the reality is that by offering forgiveness, you are freeing up yourself to be able to move forward and to stop being trapped by events of the past.

One thing that can be helpful is to begin to look at your children as great and wonderful blessings, and those blessings would never have come into your life without their father. In your mind, begin to separate your feelings for your child's father from your daily life. Every time you think of something you are angry or resentful about in regard to your past relationship, force yourself to think of something you are thankful for. This is a replacement approach to thinking that involves choosing to replace your negative thoughts with positive ones.

You have come to a place where you will no longer be a part of his life as his wife or girlfriend, so it is important you let go of the past. You, your children, and your former spouse are creating a new scenario, so it is important to build it from a place void of anger and resentment. Staying angry and bitter will not solve anything, and it will not change one iota of where you have been or what you have been through. It will only carry an unhappy spirit with you into this new life and new beginning.

Co-plan to co-parent

As you and your former husband or partner move forward to create separate lives, there will always be something that joins you: your children. You are still on the same team when it comes to being parents. Ultimately — while it may not seem like it at times — you both want what is best for your children. It is important to remember that your children are the most important factor in the equation when relating to their father.

Single Mothers Speak

Heidi Colonna, mother of six

"Having a relationship with my sons' father has been both stressful and rewarding. We have all benefitted enormously, as we have been able to maintain very open custody arrangements because we have been able to maintain civility. We alternate weeks Friday to Friday, but the boys have the option of choosing to deviate from this schedule as events arise. Because their schools are near my home, I see them daily during the week, and they often drop in at my house during the week when they stay with their Dad and during my former husband's placement time in the summer. Because we were able to maintain good communication, the boys do not have to choose between us. Instead, they get both of us.

Maintaining a civil relationship has allowed the boys opportunities that I could not have afforded on my own, as we have been able to agree on activities and share the cost of those activities that are above and beyond the normal maintenance expenses.

> *It also allows the boys the opportunity to have both parents attend their events without dreading the tension that a co-attended event might produce.*
>
> *My boys have the opportunity to see me interact with their father in a civil manner, despite our differences, which is, in and of itself, a valuable life lesson."*

The first step in making this new separate life work, for your children and for yourself, is to establish open and ongoing lines of communication. The more you communicate with their father and the least amount of emotion or anger you feel when doing so, the more that your children will be at ease and settle into their new lives. It is crucial to avoid having a child feel that he or she is in the middle of a conflict between you and his or her father.

Part of co-parenting is constant, clear communication. Say what you mean when you are discussing issues and schedules with your children's father. Do not infer things or how you feel about an issue — he is not a mind reader. It is not your former spouse's job to figure out what you are saying, so it is beneficial to everyone involved for you to be direct.

It is important to set ground rules ahead of time not just for the kids, but for you as parents. Agree with your former spouse or partner to have discussions when the children are not present about times and dates for visits. This should be done on the phone, when the kids are not present, or via e-mail so that children are not privy to what can prove, at times, to be heated discussions. While at times this may prove to be difficult, try to keep sarcasm out of your repertoire of rejoinders. While your child's father may make you angry and bring out a level of frustration in you that is so high you want to scream, you need to learn to set these feelings aside. It is important that you both remember your relationship is no longer about the two of you, but instead it is entirely about creating the best life possible for your children. Your children and their needs are paramount.

As you communicate with your child's father, make your needs clearly known. If your daughter, for example, needs to be home by 4 p.m. on a Saturday so that she can attend a birthday party, let her father know. If you are direct with your needs, you will more likely have them met. No one can meet your needs if they are not aware of what those needs are. For this reason, communicating specifics is vitally important.

By choosing to avoid communicating with your former spouse, you will not be avoiding conflict, but instead, you will be creating a breeding ground for greater conflict. Your emotions will well up as you allow unresolved issues to grow. As well, by avoiding a discussion of whatever problems exist, the problems will grow and fester instead of going away. By practicing avoidance, you will be compounding your problems. Address problems or issues with your children's father as soon as you realize they exit. Find time to speak to him when your children are not around or cannot eavesdrop on the conversation.

Do not play telephone

Children should not become little telephone operators, ferrying messages between their two parents. They should not serve as go-betweens when issues or information needs to be dispersed; that is your job as adults. This is an unsound position for them to be put it, as well as an unhealthy environment for adults to create. The more that you and your former spouse can establish open lines of communication, the healthier your relationship with each other will be on an ongoing basis. Agree between yourselves that communication — however you choose to do it — should remain between the adults, not through the children.

Lay down the law — together

While the two of you will be living separate lives and your children will ultimately be split between two homes, it is important there is a sense of unity when it comes to discipline for children. Discuss what the rules will be for your children at both houses. It is important that you and your children's father come up with a structured concept of what is allowed and what is not allowed for both households. By doing this, the children will find it much easier to transition from one house to the other. Once the rules are set, make them clear to your children, and then be sure to stick with them. Children do not just need structure; they require it.

Psychological studies have conclusively shown that children from infancy on do better emotionally when they live within the confines of a scheduled, routine life. Schedules and routines provide a sense of security and create good patterns for healthy daily living. Going to sleep, waking up, and having meals at regular times are important for children, so it is best to ensure you and your children's father agree on the schedule you will follow when your children are in each of your care. The more structure you both bring to your children's lives, the more both of you as parents can offer your children and the healthier your children will be emotionally. This will also make your parenting experience more enjoyable.

According to author and therapist Diane M. Berry, the most effective way you can help your child combat the effects of divorce is to create a stable and routine life he or she can come to rely on.

Take the High Road

It is important to remember not to say negative things about your former spouse because he is still your children's father. When you say negative things about your child's father, this does not draw your child closer to you, but instead alienates him or her from you, causing your child to feel the need to defend his or her father.

When your children share what their father has been doing, do not encourage them to do this. It is also important that you do not ask them for information; it is not their job to become your private investigators or to check up on their father for you. Keep in mind, if you create an environment that encourages them to "tattle" on their father, be assured they will feel that this is something that they should do in regard to you and your lifestyle as well.

When your former husband does something that upsets your children, do not make excuses for him. Let him explain himself to the children. Employ non-emotional responses when your children speak about their father, no matter what their reactions are. Do not let your anger show when your children tell you something that their father has said or done that you do not agree with or that makes you angry. For example, if your children tells you that they were allowed to stay up all night watching movies, despite the fact that they had stayed home sick from school the day before, instead of showing your children how angry you are, calmly listen to their recounting the events of the past weekend. If you feel the situation warrants addressing, address the issue with their father at a later date when the children are not present or cannot overhear your conversation.

Furthermore, instead of reacting in anger when you are frustrated with something your children's father has done, listen calmly and ask your children how the situation made them feel. Allow the discussion to ultimately prove to be about your children and not their father. While the discussion may begin with a child sharing something about his or her father, you can change the focus of the talk to the child's feelings and reactions instead of details about his or her father's life.

Children take their cues from their primary caregiver. They formulate their feelings and perceptions largely by judging yours as their mother. A mother's feelings — and especially her reactions — will set the tone for the household. If she is disturbed, a single mother needs to learn to express her feelings to other adults who can help and guide her in the best way of resolving or addressing those feelings.

Answering the Tough Questions

It is safe to assume that whenever your child becomes able to formulate ideas, he or she will then formulate questions, usually around when your child turns 3 years old. With this in mind, it is important that you as a mother think through the questions that your child may pose prior to them asking. Children may ask questions like, "Why don't you love Daddy anymore?" or "Why does Daddy have a new lady at his house?" Or, they may ask what they did wrong that made their Daddy go away. As well, children can question the dynamics of relationships and households they observe through friends at school. While you are ruminating on these questions, begin to formulate age-appropriate answers.

Children have an uncanny sense of timing. Your child invariably will ask you a thought-provoking question at the most inopportune time. For example, you can be driving in the car and your son may ask why his Daddy did not pick him up last night and if this means he is not loved anymore. You need to be prepared because your response will largely dictate how well your child will accept your answer. If you are emotionally overwrought, your child will take his or her cues from you and interpret this as an unsettling subject. If your child has asked whether he is still loved even though his Dad neglected to come by the house for a planned visit and you start sobbing, your child will understand that this is a terrible situation and even you cannot handle it. Respond calmly, instead saying that maybe he should give his Dad a call to make sure that everything is all right. Remain unemotional because this will prove to be a healthier response for both your child and you in the long run.

If you are too emotional to discuss some of the issues — the divorce or separation, visits with their father, why their father refuses to be involved, etc. — with your children, consider having someone who is close to them discuss their father or issues pertaining to him with them. For example, a grandparent, aunt, or uncle who they have been especially close to in the past may prove to be a good choice. Sometimes, distancing yourself from the situation until you can keep your emotions in check is a healthier option for both you and your children in the long run. This will help you avoid saying and doing things that you will come to regret once you have created some emotional distance.

Your children need to have an age-appropriate understanding of why their father is not present in the home. This understanding needs to validate the reality that their father is 50 percent of them. To do this, in all of your explanations do no criticize or malign their father. A mother who maligns an absentee father is helping erode a child's feelings about him or herself. A father — absent or present — is part of a child and when you reject a child's father, a child feels this as a personal rejection. Whether the child can relate to his or her father or not, the child will realize that there are some parts of himself or herself that are from his or her father.

For the most part, when a divorce occurs, children feel largely caught in the middle of their two parents. While you may have very negative feelings about your former spouse, most likely your children do not harbor the same ill will toward their father. For this reason, when children begin to ask questions about the divorce, tact and sensitivity to their feelings must be used.

When children begin to question why their parents are divorcing or have divorced, there oftentimes are undercurrents of anger, fear, desperation, and frustration because they:

- Are angry that life as they know it has and will change

- May fear that you will leave as their father has

- Feel a sense of desperation, as they may attempt to reverse their parents' decision to divorce and no longer be together

- May experience an overwhelming sense of frustration as they realize that their efforts to change their parents' feelings are not effective

With all this in mind, it is important to craft your answers to your child's questions with sensitivity. The first thing you should do is begin with the truth in an age-appropriate manner. Give as much detail as you think your child will be able to handle at his or her age. You know your child better than anyone else. After you have studied information on the ages and stages of children (see a website like KidsGrowth.com at **www.kidsgrowth.com/stages/guide/index.cfm**), make an informed decision about the right amount of information to give your child at his or her specific stage of development. If necessary, have separate conversations with each of your children so you can most effectively address their concerns and questions and provide age-appropriate responses.

Be honest. Make a practice of telling your children truthful answers to their questions. If you fabricate your answers and are dishonest, you will set a tone for your children, leading them to question what you tell them. Children are surprisingly aware of their circumstances and want the truth.

Speaking the truth will reassure your children and create a sense of security within them. It is important for your child to feel secure, especially at this time of great change within their lives. They may not like the answers that they are given, but children crave an environment that feels secure and honesty is the base for this security. It is also the base for all communication in the future between you and your children. If you are less than truthful with them, when it comes time for them to share details of their lives, your children will have been taught that it is acceptable to be dishonest.

When having this discussion and discussions similar to this with your children, it is important to keep in the forefront of your thoughts – before you speak – that you are not attempting to lodge a complaint with your children against their father. Your words should not in any way aim to persuade your children to believe that their father is a negative part of their lives. Do not put your children in a place where they have to choose between you and your former spouse or partner.

Single Mothers Speak

Colene Carpenter, mother of one

"I have to say that all the negative and false comments that my son's father makes about me are hurtful. I think that his saying these things is because he is attempting to cover up all his wrongdoings and put the focus back on me. To get by, I just do what I can not to let it bother me.

I am always there for my son if he has questions or wants to know about something that is going on. I try to make all the answers I give him short and sweet and to the point. Even though bad things are said about me, I make sure that I never say anything negative about his father."

Discussions with your children about their father and the evolving circumstances associated with divorce will change over the ensuing years, so keep in mind this topic should be a dialogue where both you and your children should have a voice in the discussion. Do not just listen to what your children are saying and the questions they are asking; really hear what the words, thoughts, and fears behind them are indicating. For example, when a child says that they do not care if they ever see their father again, realize that they are simply exhibiting a defense mechanism. They are rejecting their father and his presence in their life before he possibly could let them down. Or, they are rejecting him after he has rejected them by not showing up for a visit or doing something he had previously promised to do. Obviously, your child wants their father to be a presence in his or her life, even if he or she says they do not, so read beyond what your child is saying and try to determine what he or she really means.

Another important detail to recognize is that timing is everything. When your child wants to talk, you need to be willing to set aside whatever you are doing to hear them. While this is not always convenient in a hectic single mother's schedule, these times offer valuable opportunities for you to discuss what your child is feeling and give your support to him or her during this period of adjustment. It is all right to leave the dishes in the sink for the night or the laundry still in the dryer because meeting your child's needs and addressing his or her concerns is far more important than any other task you may need to attend to. Help your children understand that they are the most important part of your life. Children, when experiencing a divorce, need constant reinforcement that they are valuable to their parents and that their parents will always be there for them. Let them know you love them. Help them understand that whether they are with their father for a visit or with you, your love is constant.

Visitation

Scheduling is a valuable part of maintaining a relationship between your children and their father. Whatever your custody agreement is, let your child know what it entails and how often he or she will see or be with his or her father. For younger children, it might be a wise idea to get a calendar where you can indicate the visitation schedule.

Obviously if your former spouse is inconsistent in maintaining a visitation schedule, it may be a wiser approach to not let your child know far in advance that an upcoming visit may occur. This way your child will not plan for the visit and then become disappointed if the visit does not happen. Try to be flexible instead of rigid in accommodating your former husband's needs.

For example, if your former spouse is supposed to take the children to dinner on Wednesday but calls to say he has a meeting at work that will keep him late, try to accommodate his request to see the children on Thursday instead. Obviously, these requests must be within reason and not a weekly occurrence that entirely disregards the set visitation schedule. The reality is, the more reasonable you can be, the more these transitional times will prove to go smoothly.

According to the National Network for Child Care, the most important aspect of a visitation schedule is doing what is best for the children. Withholding a child from a visitation simply to satisfy your own purposes or because you do not want to accommodate your former spouse's schedule is not healthy for you or, more importantly, for your child. Withholding visitation does not punish your child's father; it punishes the child. Therefore, unless your child's father's requests are impossible to meet, it is best to be accommodating.

However, if you find that your former husband blatantly disregards the boundaries set out in your visitation schedule and you have discussed this with him, revert to the stipulated agreement. If he continues to violate the agreement, despite you discussing it with him, consult with the attorney who was responsible for drawing up the schedule and see what your options are. This should be your last resort. The more that you and your former spouse can resolve this issues on your own, the greater foundation you will be laying for a positive relationship in the future.

It is important to remember you cannot keep your children from having a relationship with their father simply because you do not like him. However, if he is doing things that endanger the welfare of your children or behaving in an unfit manner, you can have the court system revisit your custody or visitation agreement. Things that endanger the well-being of your children include issues of substance abuse, homelessness, reckless actions, and mental issues. Another thing that a single mother should be aware of is who their children's father is involved with and who he introduces the children to while they are with him. If your children report having been in an environment that you feel is unfit or unhealthy, checking into the validity of your children's comments is your first step in making sure your children are safe. There are times that children exaggerate events or circumstances; make sure that what your children are saying is true before you take action.

While it may seem at times that having a father figure — any male — in the picture would make things better, that is not always the case. Because of this mentality, a single mother may latch on to any male who is willing to occupy the father figure in an effort to supply this role to her family. However, studies show that a present father figure who is harmful and causes emotional damage to a child is far worse than a child who grows up in an emotionally healthy home without a father figure. Furthermore, consistent legal rulings have shown that the court systems across the nation agree that having an unfit parent involved in a child's life is not helpful but detrimental to the child's welfare. It is for this reason that involvement in a child's life can be terminated.

If your child's father is entirely out of the picture, whether because he has chosen not to be a part of your children's lives, lives out of the state, has died, or any other host of scenarios, consider facilitating a relationship with your former in-laws.

In-Laws Do Not Have to Become Outlaws

It is often difficult when you are navigating your way through a divorce to keep things on an amicable level with your former in-laws. It may seem, for some, that when a divorce occurs they will be losing half of their extended family. For others, it may be a relief to no longer have to contend with a former mother-in-law or extended family. However, it is important at this time and when establishing patterns for going forward to remember that these people will still comprise half of your child's family, no matter your feelings toward them. The amount of interaction you have with your former in-laws will largely depend on how close you were to them prior to your divorce.

Very little research has been done in support of the importance of maintaining a relationship with a single mother's former in-laws. The only consistent findings seem to be that in the event of a divorce, contact and support from the in-laws definitively drops off. Contact also seems to drop off as the children age.

It seems that the best approach for a single mother in regard to relating to her former in-laws is what is best and healthiest for her children. No two situations and relationships are the same, so how you relate to your former in-laws and how often your children see them will be largely based on what will work for and benefit your children the most. If seeing their grandparents opens them up to a hostile and hurtful environment, it is best to create some space until emotions become less volatile. If you see that time spent with their grandparents seems to be a positive addition to your children's schedule, then an effort should be made to maintain contact.

In some cases, the lack of the father's presence may even open a new avenue for a relationship with your in-laws that had not previously existed. With their father missing, your former in-laws may have more of an opportunity to become involved with your children. This, however, is up to you and them to decide what all of you can handle and accommodate. Whatever the situation, allow this time to be one where you set new and healthy precedents for an ongoing relationship with the other half of your child's family.

If you have an established relationship with your former in-laws, make every effort to maintain this relationship. When you are going through divorce proceedings, call those people who you were closest to and inform them on what your children are up to and what activities are keeping them busy. Do not broach the subject of your children's father. If your former in-laws bring up the subject of the divorce and/or your former spouse, simply say that this is a subject that you would rather not discuss because it will be awkward and uncomfortable for everyone involved. Do not say anything about your former spouse to his family. While they may love and adore you, they are still his family and ultimately their first allegiance will nearly always side with him.

When dealing with your in-laws, be prepared for the possibility of rejection. As unfortunate as this may be, your former family may feel that they have to take sides or avoid you all together. This does not always occur. However, if this should happen do not take this personally, as they are not rejecting you but simply trying to move forward in this newly established relationship. If you are comfortable doing so, try explaining that while you understand that things are not as they once were, you would like to move forward and maintain contact because it is what is best for the children. Let them know how important it is to you that your child remains in contact with them. If you allow your child to be the central focus of relating to your former in-laws, your child may be the bridge that allows you both to come together with a certain commonality. This may be uncomfortable at first, but the tensions often seem to ease with the passing of time.

Have a thick skin when dealing with your former in-laws, as they may tend to direct their feelings of displeasure with the divorce at you. Oftentimes, what they cannot say to your former husband they will spout off to you. For example, your former in-laws may express their anger that the two of you did not try harder or they may say that the two of you were not committed enough to one another. These remarks can prove to be hurtful and misdirected, so do not grant them much power in your life. Instead, try and empathize with what your in-laws are going through; they are hurting and want to express themselves, and oftentimes, they have not thought through what they are saying before they speak. In response, you may again want to reiterate that you do not want to discuss the demise of your marriage or the reasons for it, but you do want to continue a relationship for the good of your children.

Times of Celebration

Holidays and major events in your child's life cannot be avoided. These can become breeding ground for annual strife if you allow them to. You as the mother, whether you are the custodial parent or not, have a lot to do with the tone of how these events play out.

Most custody agreements map out when, where, and how long holidays will be divvied up between the two parents. Once these agreements have been reached, try to be as amicable as possible in making these arrangements. Again, keep in mind these holidays and moments of celebration should be happy events in your children's lives, not times when they witness their mother having a meltdown because she is upset about the holiday visitation schedule.

If your children have traditionally spent Christmas or a particular night of Chanukah with your husband's family, do not break with tradition, at least in the beginning of this adjustment period as your children acclimate to their new lives. Help them adjust by happily sending them on their way to a wonderful holiday celebration. If you need to cry or take a few moments to collect yourself, make sure this is done in private and not in front of your children. It is entirely normal and understandable to feel sad at times like these because these moments are an adjustment for all.

For those events, such as graduations or sporting events, where you, your children's father, and his family will be attending, be prepared that relating may be a bit awkward for all concerned, especially initially. However, do not let the fact that you may feel uncomfortable keep you from attending any event. Put your feelings aside, and focus on your child. Your child will feel more secure and encouraged when he or she knows all of his or her family, not just separate parts of it, can get along and come together just for him or her. This is important, as it reassures the child that nothing about his or her family's love has changed, just the dynamics of where each parent resides.

When you are in public, try to avoid fights or disagreements with your former spouse. Avoid discussions that may become heated. Your children will be the biggest loser in this equation if the two of you create a scene because they will suffer embarrassment. Many children may believe that they caused the argument between the two of you because you are attending an event connected to them.

For those children whose father's family instantly disappears at the time the divorce papers are signed, it is very important for a mother to create a support system and develop relationships that will be ongoing. Whether the relationships be with the mother's extended family or long-time friends, it is important to have ongoing relationships for you and your children to rely on. *Developing this support system and these types of ongoing relationships will be discussed in detail in Chapter 9.*

When All Else Fails

When you feel you have exhausted every avenue in trying to reach a place of peace when relating to your children's father, if he is unwilling to make smooth transitions for your children or if he continually disregards established boundaries for your children, it is time to involve a third party. A mediator or a family counselor is a wise choice to help you walk through these troublesome times. Choosing a mediator to referee your differences is just coming into greater popularity. Traditionally, couples ironed out divorce proceedings with a lawyer and then consulted with a counselor when they had trouble relating to one another. However, now it seems a much more common practice to have a mediator carry the family though the divorce and the resulting ongoing issues.

Mediators or a family counselor offer an unbiased view, which will help iron out issues that may have developed. What they will attempt to do is sort through the rubble and create a fair arrangement that you will all follow. These mediators can help with scheduling or help establish communication lines between two parents. These professionals can also provide guidance as to how best to co-parent even though you are no longer a married couple.

When our anger builds up, our defenses go up with it, making it more difficult for us to compromise. As a single mother who is trying to establish her home and sort through her feelings, this can be a very stressful time. Often, this stress can lead to overly emotional reactions, which do not help the situation but instead further deteriorate it. Using the services of a counselor or mediator can provide an unbiased opinion that can decrease the gap between the two parents. Often, the lawyer you used during your divorce proceedings can provide you with a list of the names of local mediators or family counselors who specialize in this type of constructive guidance. For those women who have not been through a divorce, mediators are readily available through local court systems.

Issues should be addressed at the earliest point possible, because if they are not handled swiftly, the anger and resentment from each parent will seep over into the lives of the children. This is harmful not only in the current situation, but it can prove to be detrimental as a child matures and becomes an adult.

Do not feel that you have failed if you seek out help. Instead, realize that you are taking the steps to be the best mother you can possibly be for your children. While some single mothers struggle through working with their children's fathers, others battle the brokenness of children whose father has abandoned his parental responsibility.

When Daddy Disappears

If your relationship with your significant other ends, it becomes apparent that your children's father is going to be an absentee father, the best thing you can do is to prepare yourself. At first, it might seem that you have to tackle the problem head on and tell your children. In most circumstances, this is not the right approach. You need to come to terms with this turn of events before you can ever hope to help your children cope with the sudden loss of their father. You also need to give the children's father time to sort through his own feelings. He may change his mind about being involved with the children after some time has passed and he has some distance from the situation and circumstances. Instead of telling your children the day after their father leaves that he has said he never wants to see them again, give the situation time to sort itself out and give your children's father the opportunity to make his own explanations.

Single Mothers Speak
Tracy Faith, mother of one

"My son's father left and never returned. I didn't become a single mother by choice. But, I have now seen that there are benefits to our unique circumstances, I get to parent my son on my own. There are no inconsistencies in the parenting, and no one fights me over how to parent."

The first thing you should do is address your feelings. If you have not dealt with your emotions in regard to your former spouse or partner's absence, you will not be able to address your child's feelings about this problem. If you are angry, disappointed, and controlled by your emotions, your children will sense this. If you feel and appear overwhelmed, your children will sense this as well and not feel safe and secure that you can handle the situation without their dad. If you need to, talk to someone about what you are experiencing. It is understandable to feel angry, disappointed, and hurt because your former partner is shirking his responsibilities as a father to the children you share. But, you need to rid yourself of these emotions so you will be a firm foundation your children can turn to as they begin to piece their new lives together.

This can be the stage when you realize that being a single mother is not all about you but instead is about raising a child who is emotionally healthy and whole. As a single mother, and now the only involved parent, you will be largely responsible for how well your child accepts this new turn of events. Your actions and reactions will set the tone for how your child responds to this because children largely take their cues of how to adjust to situations from their parents. It is important for you to set the standard for their reaction. If your children recognize that you are miserable about this turn of events and you are emotionally overwrought and cannot handle this new lifestyle, they too will not be able to handle the loss of their father from their lives.

Start by listening to your children. Hear how they feel and listen to what they are not saying. If they are very clingy, realize they need more assurance from you that you will be there for them; tell them that you are not going anywhere. If your usually docile child is acting out at day care or at school, take notice of this as well. Many times, children do not even realize how much their emotions are affecting them and do not have the ability to talk through these feelings. A helpful resource when attempting to understand your children and their emotions during this time of great change is **http://kidshealth.org**. This site offers explanations on how to deal with children at a specific age and the emotional responses often associated with that specific age. Understanding these specifics allows a parent to be better equipped at dealing with each child's specific needs.

Realize that some of these feelings of hurt and anger may spill out on to you. Your children may even blame you for their father no longer being around. While this is hurtful, do not take it personally. Approach them by saying that you realize how very much they are hurting because their father is not around. Tell them you understand why they are upset or even angry. However, in broaching this subject, it is important not to say anything about how terrible it is that their father left them or that their father is simply a bad person. Whether he is absent or present, your children's father is still a part of your children and talking badly about him will lower their feelings about themselves and encourage low self-esteem. Instead, just let them know that you understand their pain.

Do not make promises to your children regarding their father that you cannot keep. Do not promise, for example, that their father will be at their birthday party or will return in time for a specific event. This is out of your control and something that you should not promise your child on behalf of their father. It is his choice to make commitments or promises. It is also important that you not give your child false hope that his or her father will return. If your child's father fails to return after you have promised that he will, your child will not only feel betrayed by his or her father's failure to appear, but they will also feel betrayed by the failure of your promise as well.

Simply explain that for now their father has chosen not to be involved. The greatest aid to your children is to consistently reiterate that your children's father's decision to leave is not about them and that you love them and will not stop loving them.

Your children's father's level of involvement may change in the future or it may not, but let your children know that this is not up to you; it is up to their father. When you are discussing your child's father's absence, make a point to listen more than you talk. Do not lie about the circumstances surrounding his leaving. If you know information, share it with your children in an age appropriate manner. For example, if your child begins to fear that his or her father is not around because he has come to some harm and you know that he is simply choosing not to be involved, make your child aware that his or her father is physically fine but is, for the time, choosing to stay away. Share only the facts with your child, and do not share an emotionally powered version of what has transpired.

When you realize that the discussion is coming to a close, re-assure your children by encouraging them and pointing out positive attributes or qualities that you have been noticing in them. You want to pour back positive feelings into their minds and hearts at a time when they obviously will be feeling rejection and a loss of love.

Along with providing for your children emotionally, a single mother may find providing for her children financially a daunting task. The more you know about your financial affairs, the better you will be able to provide for your children's future and your own.

Chapter 6

The Green Giant — Financial Affairs

According to the U.S. Census Bureau, approximately 84 percent of parents who have custody of their children are mothers and roughly 79 percent of those mothers are employed outside of the household. About 29 percent of single

> *"It feels uncommonly queer to have enough cash to pay one's own bills. I'd have sold my soul for it a few years ago!"*
>
> — Edith Wharton
>
> *Pulitzer prize-winning American writer*
>
> *January 4, 1862 – August 11, 1937*

mothers work part-time or part of the year. With that said, nearly one-third of all single mothers live below the poverty level, and of that third, only 6 percent receive Temporary Assistance for Needy Families or TANF. TANF is a federal assistance program that provides temporary assistance to qualifying families while bringing aid and directives to them in their job search. Qualification for the program is based on family income, available resources, and the absence of child support funds. While TANF can be a supplement to help single mothers through a difficult time in their lives, the single most important thing that a single mother can do is increase her earnings or quality of employment, reports the U.S. Department of Health and Human Services.

One of the greatest gifts you can give to your children is financial security. Once you have secured a job that gives you consistent income, it is time to focus on becoming financially secure. While your children may not be old enough to understand what a bank account is, your financial security will affect them. Financial security will offer you and your children a better life, both now and for years to come. Ultimately, this financial soundness will create a more harmonious and happy home due to a lowered stress level. Studies show that one of the largest contributors of stress for a single mother is lack of adequate financial resources.

According the U.S. Census Bureau, approximately 79 percent of single mothers are gainfully employed. Unfortunately, 27 percent of single mothers and their children live at the poverty level. The Urban Institute reports that families with two parents — whether both parents are employed or not — have more than twice the income resources as those of single parent families. However, reality is that a lack of funds is one of the greatest stressors for any household, not just single mothers. This is not to advocate that money brings or buys happiness. However, an adequate income and secure financial foundation allows a single mother to live a less stressful life and affords more opportunities for her children.

Single Mothers Speak

Helena Grant, mother of three

"As a single mother, my biggest challenge was that there was never enough money to support myself and the children. I was awarded only $400 a month by the courts in child support. That really was not enough to support two children. So, I cut coupons and constantly checked out ways to get more for less. Even the kids helped out. They thought it was really cool to figure out ways to cut costs and then see the money add up that we had saved. They learned to do with not having candy or ice cream or those things that kids usually ask for. When it came time for Christmas, we didn't have a tree and each of my kids got only three presents. That was all I could afford, that year. I know it was hard on them, but it was even harder on me watching them do without. It took a great deal of work and perseverance to become financially stable. Providing the things my children needed became my focus. I eventually realized all my goals, and I continue to set goals and obtain them, both as a mother and as a woman."

As a mother, one of the most important things you can do is garner an understanding and knowledge of financial affairs. Because you are now a single mother and the new head of your household, it is imperative to have an understanding of financial matters. Taking stock of your finances is admittedly the most tedious part of the process of becoming financially sound, but it is truly the most important.

Throughout this chapter, you will be guided through the process of taking stock of your finances. Without this, you will not be able to move forward successfully. If you are not aware of you financial state, you will not be able to address those issues of weakness and build for the future. Three of the most important ways you can build for the future are eliminating any debt you may have, creating a saving plan that is best for you, and purchasing a life insurance policy. To accomplish these three things, the first thing you should do is come to an accurate understanding of where you are financially.

Take Stock

The first step in putting your financial affairs in order is to have a clear idea of what your financial standing is. Take stock of your financial standing by determining how much money you have in the bank, and then take an account of what your monthly finances entail. To do this, you will need to take note of how much money you earn monthly, what amount you spend on expenses, and how much money you are saving. These amounts need to be accurate because the more that you guess and estimate on amounts, the less you will know about your financial standing.

Look at your monthly income — your take-home pay or spousal support check — and tabulate the exact amount you have as income. Then, calculate the amount of money you have currently residing in investments. For example, if you have a life insurance policy, include this within the amount of money you are adding up. After this, list your debts and monthly expenditures.

Make three separate calculations: one for income, one for expenses, and a third for ongoing debt. These are for your own personal use, so be honest with yourself. As you tabulate, when in doubt tend to underestimate monthly income and do not inflate your income, as this may leave you at a deficit each month. When you are counting up expenses, lean toward the most amount of money you will spend monthly, not the least. The third column, which is the one where you are tallying your current debt, will be addressed further along in this chapter.

Once you are aware of what your expenses really are, you will have the ability to make accommodations and to trim expenses that will help you save money. Managing your finances is an essential skill that can be learned.

Create a Manageable Budget

A budget is a spending plan that shows how anticipated income will be allocated to cover all anticipated expenses. Budgeting allows you to be in control of your money instead of allowing your money — or lack of it — to control you. To create a budget, you will need all the information you have used to take stock of your finances regarding your income, expenses, and debt.

One website that offers a printable budget form is BetterBudgeting.com (**www.betterbudgeting.com**). Many people find it much easier to follow an outline when figuring a budget. This website offers a number of different forms so that you will be able to find one that best meets your needs.

Divide your expenses into two different categories: one category for fixed expenses that remain the same from month to month (a mortgage payment or a car payment) and the other category is for variable expenses that will change from month to month and are not ongoing (like gifts and entertainment options). Add up both your income and your expenses. If your income is higher than your expenses, you are on the right track with your budget. If you have discovered that your expenses out number your income, you need to refigure where you are spending your money each month and make some cuts. The best place to initially make cuts in your expenses is to look at the category of variable expenses. Can you cut down on eating out or going to the movies? What about spending less on gifts?

Another thing you can do to help keep your budget in check is to prioritize your expenses. This will allow you to see what you must spend money on and what expenses you can do without. As you are making cuts in your budget, take those items off your budget that are at the lowest level of priority. Continue to make cuts in your budget until your income exceeds your expenses. If it is impossible to make your income exceed your expenses, it is time to consider that you are going to need a larger supply of financial resources or to consider making substantial changes in your living arrangements in an effort to cut costs. Moving to a smaller apartment can provide economic relief, as can turning in a more expensive car you are leasing for a less expensive model. This will allow for more money coming in versus going out. As well, consider moving closer to work to decrease your commute or look into other job opportunities that would increase your income; however, do not leave a job until you are assured that you have a new position.

After you have a working budget in place, it is important to examine your budget each month. After the first few months, you may even want to make adjustments if you see that you have allocated more or less than you need in certain areas. One way to track your expenses is by using a computer program. Microsoft Money and Quicken are two of the more common programs that are used for tracking your personal budget. These programs allow you to input your expenses and then they follow your monthly spending without the hassle of ongoing calculations.

Another common way of tracking expenses is to keep a running tally within your checkbook. Whether you are writing a check or using a debit card, keeping a constant count on what is going out and what is coming in is a wise idea. Some people find that taking a few minutes at the end of each day to log all expenses helps them keep an accurate tally. As well, it allows them to not forget to include small expenses that at a later date may be forgotten.

Another option is to hire an accountant or financial advisor, if you have the economic resources to do so. Ask those you see as being economically successful who they use. Then, once you have a list of a few accountants, interview them.

See if their approach fits your approach to saving and investing. Ask about their experience, who their clients generally are, and what economic range their clients tend to fall into. Accountants charge a range of fees depending on the services they will be providing. Some accountants charge an hourly rate, while others bill according to the service they are providing.

If you do not have the financial resources to pay for an accountant to help with revenue strategies, one website you can visit is **http://free-financial-advice.net** hosted by Free Financial Advice. This website can be a starting place to find directed help to get you on your way to being financially sound, and it will also provide a starting point for locating low-cost help for financial advice.

Are you finding it hard to stick with you budget once you have created it? One option you can consider is cash envelopes.

Cash envelopes

A great way to force yourself to adhere to the budget you have created is the cash envelope system. This is a simple and free system that helps you learn to budget and be accountable with allocated funds. As a single mother, you are solely accountable to yourself because there will be no one looking over your shoulder or checking up on you to make sure that you are staying within your budget.

Cash envelopes create a system by which you can clearly monitor yourself. At the beginning of the month, divvy up cash for each section of your budget. For example, if you have budgeted $300 a month for groceries, place $300 in an envelope dedicated to your grocery fund. Then, when you head to the grocery store, grab some cash from the envelope and return the change to the envelope when your shopping trip is complete. This will cause you to quickly become aware of budgeting. When the envelope is empty, do not allow yourself to dip into your bank account or savings. Instead, force yourself to plan your spending more strategically the next month.

People who employ the cash envelope system do not have to keep large sums of money for all their expenses in their home. Money for large monthly bills will still routinely be kept in the bank, while the allotted money for other expenses will be kept on hand for groceries, gas, children's lunches, and other incidentals. When you are using the cash envelope system, the cash you have allotted for your mortgage payment, for example, would not need to be kept in an envelope because it is a regular amount and would not be something that you could spend too much money on in one month. Expenses that are routinely paid by check or online banking do not need to be relegated to an envelope, as they are a fixed and regular amount.

Conversely, if you find that you always have extra cash at the end of the month in certain envelopes, you will quickly realize that you have over budgeted in these areas. Make a commitment to yourself to put leftover money in a savings account at the end of the month or create a rewards system for yourself. For example, when there is money left over at the end of the month in the food budget, treat yourself and your children to a meal out.

Cutting Expenses

There are many ways anyone can cut their expenses; all you need is a bit of planning and some thought. Cutting expenses can become a challenging game, if you make it that way. See how much you can save each month by keeping a running tally, and then see if you are able to save more money the following month.

Food expenses

There are a number of ways to cut your food bills — whether they are grocery bills or your food bill at a restaurant. Strategic shopping, a bit of planning, and using coupons are just a few plans you can implement to lower your bills.

Many restaurants offer coupons that reduce the cost of your meal or buy one get one free deals. Sometimes, there are specified days that the offer is only good on or between certain hours of the day, for example early bird specials. These specials are offered on dinner meals served prior to the traditional dinner times, which usually happens before 5 p.m. This may be optimum for moms with young children. Some restaurants offer free children's meals on designated days of the week. Check to see what days of the week these deals run, keeping in mind that many times, these deals are not offered on weekends. Keep your eyes open for new restaurants in your area because many newly opened restaurants offer incentives to entice customers to the new restaurant.

The key with all these offers, incentives, and coupons is to make sure that you read the fine print before arriving at the restaurant. Discovering that you are not there on the right day or at the right time to use the coupon or get the special defeats the savings can be frustrating.

Another way to save on your food budget is to cut out junk food and fast food. While stopping at a fast food chain can prove to be a time saver, it is not a money saver. Fast food and junk food are more expensive than food prepared at home, and they are also healthier alternatives for snacking. Making this change is a win-win situation for a mother because she will be able to save money and provide her family with healthier food.

Aside from cutting out junk food, selectively shopping can help reduce a monthly grocery bill. Certain stores offer more competitive prices on items than other stores, so with a bit of shopping around, it will be easy to determine which store offers the best prices on meats, vegetables, canned goods, and other items you might buy on a regular basis. Also, strategically shopping can help lower expenditures. Purchasing items when they are on sale by perusing the weekly sales circulars can make a big difference. Consider planning your menu around the sale items for the week. You can also cut coupons for savings. Coupons are offered in a variety of places including newspapers and circulars. There are even entire websites devoted to issuing cost-cutting coupons for all types of items. Go to Coupons.com (**www.coupons.com**) or to CoolSavings (**www.coolsavings.com**) to get started on using coupons to reduce spending. Or, check out Billeater.

com (**http://billeater.com**), which offers money-saving tips and coupons. Another site to visit is Groupon (**www.groupon.com**), which sends you an area-specific coupon each day via e-mail.

It is important to remember when you are clipping coupons and looking for sales to be sure that you are purchasing those items that you really need and will use. Do not simply purchase something because you happen to find a great deal on it or you have a coupon in hand. That item will end up in the back of your pantry, unused, and will eventually be a waste of precious money. Also, consider not having meat at every dinner because meat is one of the most costly things purchased on grocery shopping trips. Eggs, beans, and cheeses can serve as a small source protein in place of meat. If you are going to purchase meat, consider doing so in bulk, which consistently offers lower prices. After you shop, divvy up the meat into portions that are right for your needs and freeze them. This will not only save you time later on, but it will also reduce your trips to the grocery store, thus reducing your grocery bill. Every mother knows that even when you head to the grocery for one item, you always leave with far more than just that one thing you went in for.

Reducing frivolous spending

Another thing you can do to reduce your budget is to cut out unnecessary expenses. For example, stop buying coffee at your favorite shop and instead make your coffee before heading out in the morning. If you spend $4 per day on coffee at your local coffeehouse, that totals $20 per week. After a year, you would have spent $1,040 on coffee, not including any weekend trips for a latte. That much money could be spent on a vacation for you and your children or used for rent or mortgage payments.

Another easy way to save money is to visit your local public library as opposed to buying your books from a bookstore or online. Libraries offer a host of resources besides books, including activities for both children and adults that are often free or offered at a reduced cost. Also, many libraries offer a selection of DVDs that can be rented for a few days or up to a week at no cost to anyone with a library card. You can eliminate rental fees and late fees simply by making a visit to the library a weekly event with your children. You can even turn a trip to the library into a quiet respite of time to yourself if you need some time for reflection or just time away from the hassles of daily life.

Another way to trim your expenses is to shop smarter when you are about to make big purchases. Do a little research when buying big ticket items such as a television or an appliance. See which item will offer you the most for your money. To do this, check out what each appliance offers and remember that some appliances have dual functions. For example, some televisions have a built in DVD player. Or, if you are purchasing a gaming system for your children, you may be able to forgo a DVD player if that system also has the ability to play DVDs. These are all things that you can learn prior to making a purchase simply by doing a bit of research.

You should also consult Consumer Reports before making a purchase. Items that do not need constant maintenance will save money in the long run and Consumer Reports offers a detailed analysis of commonly purchased items, including cars. Consumer Reports offers a monthly subscription magazine or you can go to their website, **www.consumerreports.org**. This organization's reports can provide direction and help you become a more discerning shopper.

Cutting down on bills

Another way to combat paying high costs for big ticket items is to buy an item on sale. Choose an item and then wait until that item is offered at a discount. You should also check the Internet for lower prices. Using a search engine you are familiar with, do a search for the item you want. Check and compare prices for the item once you have located it. Another possibility for price cutting is to go directly to the website of the product's manufacturing company because, oftentimes, ordering directly can save you money. As well, waiting for an item to go on sale helps in two ways. It allows you to see if you really want the item badly enough to wait until the price lowers, and it causes you to think through purchases and reduce the chance of impulse buying.

The next place you should look to for cutting money is your monthly cable bill. When money is tight, it is time to evaluate whether you really need premium movie channels or additional channels that cost more than a basic cable package. You can also check into consolidating your bills. If you have a cable provider, will they also include phone and Internet service at a reduced cost when you subscribe to all three services? While checking into these options, also consider cutting down on the phone services you have.

Do you need a landline and cell phone, or could you do without a landline? Or, could you do without all the additional options you have on your cell phone and your children's cell phones? If you need to text or send data, do you need to have unlimited texting or data options? Do your children go over their texting limits each month, causing you to incur overage fees? These are all questions you need to ask yourself and then answer before going another month with expenses that you could easily reduce. Also, before you renew your cell phone plan, check to see if your provider now is offering a plan that would be more cost effective for your needs than the one you currently have in place. Cell phone companies are constantly changing plans, and an uneducated shopper will simply renew their plan without questioning possible savings. Be an educated shopper and shop around for the best option you can find.

Next, examine your gas and electric bills. Call both companies and see if they offer reduced cost plans. Many companies now offer budget programs designed to fit your usage needs while reducing your costs. As well, consider making more of an effort to lower your monthly bill at home. The following are simple suggestions for ways to lower your utility bills:

- Turn off lights when you leave a room, turn off electronic devices when you or your children are not using them, and if you watch televisions before you get into bed, make sure you set a sleep timer so the television turns off after a certain period of time.

- Purchase energy efficient bulbs to reduce your electrical bill.

- See if you can set your thermostat to an "away" setting if no one is at home during the day because there is no point to running air conditioning or heat if no one is home.

- Instead of turning the air conditioning on, open a window. Or, in the autumn months, instead of turning the heat on, put an extra blanket on your bed at night to stay warm.

- Reduce your monthly water bill by doing consistent maintenance on all your faucets. A leaky faucet is not just annoying when it drips loudly, but it is also counting out the pennies you are wasting each time a drop of unused water falls.

Becoming a bargain diva

While this may not go over well with your children, visit thrift stores. To make purchasing used items more palatable, make it an adventure to search out the best buys at a thrift store. Many times, you can find unworn clothing with tags still on them that are half the cost of the item at a department store. As an incentive to your children, suggest that if you can save a specified amount of money, they will have the opportunity to choose a more expensive item off of their list to buy.

Think negotiating a price is cheap and tacky? Think again. Negotiating and bargaining to get you what you want saves money. While you may not be aware of this, even big name department stores will haggle over prices in today's economy in hopes of exacting a sale. Stores that offer appliances and electronic devices are best known for their willingness to negotiate prices. Clothing stores that have recently held a sale or are going to in a few days will often be willing to offer you the sale price to ensure the sale. Go in with a price in mind and know what you are willing to spend before you even begin to bargain. Ask to speak to a manager if a clerk says that he or she is not authorized to offer you a better deal. Do not be embarrassed by haggling over a price; instead, make it a game where you come away the winner.

Another step you can take is to examine your hygiene. How much are you paying for trips to the salon? Do you get your nails done each week? Could you switch from a costly name brand shampoo to a generic brand? These are questions only you can answer. Keep in mind that while you want to save money, do so in a way that you can handle. Do not make so many abrupt changes to your lifestyle that you and your children are left miserable and uncomfortable. Try to make these changes as positive as possible for all of you.

Hold an exchange

If you want the latest fashions but do not have the money to buy the new things you or your children want, or you are tired of wearing the same old thing again and again, plan an exchange. The exchange can be just clothing or can include accessories, handbags, and even shoes. Invite friends and family to bring barely used clothing. Keep track of how many items each person brings with them. Allow each person to exchange their items for something someone else is offering.

Once you have tried these and other strategic spending and saving plans and you have a working budget in place, it is important to address debt if you have it.

Rid Yourself of Debt

If after all your calculations you realize that you have accrued debt, this is the first financial aspect you need to examine. Do not be too hard on yourself if you are in debt. The approximate credit card debt per household is $10,691 in the United States. This estimate does not factor in other types of debts a household may have.

What is your debt? Is it a mortgage? Is it a car? Or, is your debt related to credit cards? It is important to figure out exactly where you owe money so that you meet minimum monthly payments and at no time fall behind in payments, which damages your credit score.

Credit cards cripple many single mothers when it comes to debt. When times get tight, many people — not just single mothers — resort to charging their purchases when they do not have available cash. More than 85 percent of all those people filing for bankruptcy do so because of credit card debt. About 43 percent of all Americans spend more than they earn each year. They largely do so by employing the use of credit cards to finance their purchases.

When cash is not in a steady supply in a single mother's life, one of the costliest mistakes a single mother can resort to is relying on credit cards, because a single mother can quickly find herself unintentionally overloaded with credit card debt. Keep in mind the single largest way that credit cards make money is when you do not pay off your monthly balance. They also make money when you only make the required monthly payment.

Until you pay off the bill in its entirety, the monthly balance grows, whether you use the card that month or not. Here are some important questions to ask yourself to assess your credit card situation:

- Is there a high balance on your existing credit cards?

- Has this balance existed for more than six months?

- Do you simply pay the monthly minimum balance?

After you have asked yourself these questions, notice how many you have answered "yes" to. If you have answered "yes" to any of these questions, you need to address this situation. By maintaining a high balance on existing credit card bills, you will pay out far more than you have charged. If you have maintained an existing balance for more than six months, you are accruing additional fees and charges without ever using your credit card for additional expenses. Each month you do not pay on your bill, you will be charged a fee. This fee usually starts at $25, but it can be more depending on how much you owe on the card. The interest rate and the additional charges will range, depending on the card and its specific terms and fees. And, if you simply pay the minimum monthly balance, you may end up paying close to three times the amount of the original charge.

The first way to way to avoid resorting to relying on credit cards for anything other than an emergency is to get rid of all your cards but two. Choose to keep the two that employ the smallest amount of interest and offer the best financial incentives to card holders and keep these cards active.

Specialty stores and department stores that issue their own cards often have the highest interest rates. Also, check to see which cards mandate an annual fee for card holders. Cards that charge an annual fee versus ones that do not are also ones that you should choose not to keep. Always maintain at least two active credit cards at all times because as you make timely monthly payments, your credit score will consistently improve. Once you have chosen which credit cards to keep, cut up the others so they are not a temptation for future use. Obviously, you will still be required to pay the bills on the credit cards you choose not to keep active, as not using them does not eliminate the accrued debt. These cards need to be paid off to reduce existing debt; cutting them up simply helps reduce the possibility of future spending.

Here is an interesting incentive to ridding yourself of the additional credit cards you hold: The more credit cards that you carry in your name, the more likely you are to be the victim of identity theft.

Next, with the remaining cards in hand, call the companies that issued the cards and negotiate lower interest rates to help you pay off these cards at a quicker rate by reducing your monthly fees. With lower interest rates in place, more of the money you are paying the companies will go toward eradicating your existing credit card debt instead of paying off interest you may have incurred. Credit card companies are more willing to negotiate lower interest rates for those who consistently pay their bills on time. Call the company and explain that while you have been a customer for some time, you are unhappy with the service they are providing. Tell the company that you see that there are credit card companies that consistently offer lower rates than the interest rate your credit card company currently offers you. Ask if there is anything that they can do about this. If you do not get a favorable reply from the first person you speak to, ask to speak to a manager. Oftentimes, the initial representative you speak to does not have the authority to make these changes in your bill.

To rid yourself of credit card debt, one of the most important steps you can take is avoid ever missing a payment. If you miss a payment, the fees that you will be charged are exorbitant. The starting cost average for a missed payment is an additional $25 tacked onto your bill. Traditionally, companies add this additional charge onto the month's next minimum required payment. When you incur late fees, your credit will be affected and this will be counted against you. Credit card companies want you to make payments because when you fail to make monthly payments, they are losing money. Often, if you call your credit card company and explain that you are diligently trying to pay off your bill, they may be willing to work with you by lowering your monthly interest rate.

As well, if you are more than 90 days in arrears — meaning you have not made a payment in this time — you may be able to negotiate a settlement with the credit card company for your existing balance. These settlements range from 20 to 75 percent of the existing balance, which means that you will be required to pay off a smaller percentage of your bill. Additionally, if you are able to pay off the debt in a lump sum, credit card companies will often reduce the amount you owe even further. This is a win-win situation for you and the credit card company. If you were to entirely default on your bill, the company would never receive any payment; however if you pay a lump sum, the company receives some payment rather than none and you have reduced your debt and bills.

The best time to contact credit card companies is at the end of the month. This is when they tend to be more willing to compromise because they want to meet their numbers and quotas regarding collections. Document the time of your call and with whom you are speaking each time you call a creditor. At the conclusion of your conversation, if you have reached an agreement or made any changes to your existing payment schedule, make sure to request that all changes be documented and sent to you.

Then take the next step and consolidate your credit card debt. This will allow you to make one payment per month, and it will also prove to lower your monthly interest rates. However, when consolidating credit card debt, do so with caution. Check any and all fees and fine print in regard to transferring balances. Make sure that you are going to be able to pay off the consolidated bill within the stipulated amount of time or you may end up with a larger debt than you started with due to raised interest rates.

Should you choose not to consolidate your credit card debt or you do not have the option to do so, begin by paying off the credit card with the highest interest rate, as this card will be the one costing you the most money over time. Choosing to pay off your debts with the highest interest rate first will allow you to begin saving at a quicker rate. High interest rate debt is like throwing money out the window because it is simply blowing away with nothing accomplished or garnered through its use.

You should aim to pay off your credit card debt before you focus on saving. The money that you are losing by continuing to support your debt is detrimental to your financial standing. When you pay off credit card bills, you will feel a huge sense of accomplishment and you will also feel that you have gotten yourself out from under a weighty burden. Once you have paid off a monthly balance, instead of taking the money you have been paying out each month and adding it to your monthly budget, try putting it into a savings account. This often offers a single mother an easy way to transition into consistent savings.

Creating Savings

It is not always easy to begin saving, but to make it more manageable, start out small. For example, begin each week by taking all of your change and putting it in one place. At the end of each month, take the change you have accrued to a converting station, which can be found in many banks and large retail store locations, and have it sorted and counted. Instead of spending this money, deposit it into a savings account. While this amount may at first seem small, it will help you establish a habit of saving.

One way to create savings without having to do a thing is to choose a bank that contributes to your savings account monthly. For example Bank of America offers a program known as Keep the Change. With this program, when you use your debit card to make a purchase, the amount of the purchase is rounded up to the nearest dollar. The difference between your purchase price and the amount your transaction is rounded up to is transferred into your savings account. For example, if you paid $4.13 for a latte, the bank would actually charge you $5 for the purchase and place the difference between the two prices (in this case 87 cents) automatically into your savings account. While initially this may not seem like much, it can start you on the road to savings. As an incentive, for the first three months that you have an active account with Bank of America, they will match your Keep the Change savings. After that, they will continue to match it by a 5 percent increase to your account annually.

Savings are imperative for long-term goals and also in the event of an emergency. Creating savings is one of the wisest financial strategies a single mother can implement in her life. Many single mothers find that it is not the day-to-day living that economically stresses them out but the cash emergencies that plague their bank accounts and then places them in a constant state of worry.

Single Mothers Speak

Tracy Faith, *mother of one*

"One of my most reassuring accomplishments is that I have a 401(k) plan and an IRA in place. This will help create a more secure future for me and for my son."

Life Insurance

While it is not a pleasant thought, as a single mother you need to prepare for your children's future in the event that something should happen to you. Life insurance (and a will stipulating where and how your money should be allocated) needs be in place. It is imperative that you take care of this as soon as you are financially able.

The reality is that historically women have been radically uninsured. According to New York Life, 59 percent of women carry some life insurance. However, the average death benefit for men is nearly double the amount compared to women who carry policies. Single mothers need to have life insurance policies to ensure the well-being of their children. Life insurance is a protection policy with a purpose of paying off existing mortgages, college tuitions, and accrued debt in the event of the policy holder so that children are not left penniless and with a looming debt.

When purchasing life insurance, it is suggested that the amount of your policy be 20 times the annual income you would desire to supplement. In other words, multiply your current annual salary by 20 to determine the amount of life insurance you should purchase. The reason for this is that if something should happen to you, you would want to make sure that your children will be financially taken care of until they reach adulthood. However, it is important to be aware that children should not be named as beneficiaries of life insurance policies, as a minor is not legally able to inherit money.

Admittedly, it is difficult for any mother to think of not being available for her children because something has happened to her. However, it is wise to think carefully about who you would like to be the administrator of your child's funds from a life insurance policy. Consider those people who you foresee being a consistent part of your child's life. Oftentimes, it is wise to choose the person you have named as children's legal guardian in your will, as the beneficiary for your life insurance policy.

Avoiding Scams

There are no easy ways to come into money. If someone promises to make you $100,000 in a week, or if they promise you can make thousands of dollars a month by working part-time in your pajamas, consider the possibility that the person may be facilitating a scam. These scam perpetrators seek out people who they know are facing economic struggles. The reality is that there are no get-rich schemes out there that work, so do not get taken in by anyone who offers you money for nothing. If something seems too good to be true, it probably is.

Ask for Advice

If you are not financially savvy and you find that your finances — or lack thereof — are beating you up, ask for help. First, seek out a close friend or family member who you know is fiscally sound and who you believe makes wise financial judgments. Ask him or her to sit down and go over your finances with you. If you need to, ask if you can be accountable to them until you get to a place where you are secure in making your own financial decisions. Request that the two of you monitor your finances, whether on a weekly or monthly basis, until you feel that you are at a place where you are comfortable taking over control.

If you have the finances but the not the savvy to know what to do with them, hire a financial planner. A financial planner will lead you through cash flow strategies, savings plans, planning for your child's educational needs, and saving for retirement. They will provide direction, help you understand the financial world to a degree where you can make wise decisions, and help you plan your financial future.

One place that can be of help in locating a financial planner is Primerica (**www.primerica.com**). If you visit the company's site, you will find an interact guide to walk you through finding a financial planner within your area. It offers a variety of services and financial options. The company's services include programs to help you become debt free as well as guidance in crating savings and a plan for your financial future.

As a mother, you want to provide a sound financial future for your son or daughter, grab every resource that will help you do this, and move forward. As you move forward financially as a single mother, you will also see that you will need to learn to navigate not just within the financial world but also the world of males and females. As we all know, there are differences between males and females, and not just physically. Effectively mothering boys versus girls has as much of a learning curve as learning to balance a check book and becoming a personal finance wizard. Effectively parenting your son or your daughter can be done, but it takes a bit of understanding and thought.

Chapter 7

Sons & Daughters —

Ages, Stages, Gender Roles, and Issues

Ages and Stages: What to Expect at Each Stage

The five stages of childhood have been defined as infancy, toddlerhood, preschool, middle childhood, and adolescence. Each stage is unique and brings with it a learning experience for both you and your child. Each child will pass

> *"So when the great word 'Mother!' rang once more, I saw at last its meaning and its place; not the blind passion of the brooding past, But Mother — the World's Mother — come at last, to love as she had never loved before — to feed and guard and teach the human race!"*
>
> *— Charlotte Perkins Gilman*
> *American sociologist and writer*
> *July 3, 1860 – August 17, 1935*

through a distinct stage similarly to other children but not exactly the same. Every child will learn to roll over, to sit up, to walk and talk, and many other things along the way, but it will differ among children and at what age and rate they acquire the ability to do these things and many others.

For example, some children distinctly learn to crawl and employ this mode of transportation until they successfully learn to walk. This same child may learn to walk between the age of 11 and 13 months. While another child may lean to walk at 9 months and entirely bypass the crawling stage all together. Neither child is right or wrong in their development; they are simply different.

As a mother, if you are parenting more than one child, you will surely be able to attest to the reality of this. Your first child, while similar to the second child in many ways, has their own unique time schedule and learning schedule. The two basic factors that influence the development of a child are genetics and environment. Both prove equally important but are vastly different.

Genetic traits are passed on to a child prior to birth, and come from the inherited combination of the mother and the father's traits. These traits include, but are not limited to, hair color, eye color, height, and stature. Personality and temperament, while influenced by outside sources, are largely determined before the birth of a child.

Environment plays a grand role in the development of who a child becomes. Environmental factors that influence the development of a child are too numerous to list, but in a simplified version, they include the location where a child grows up, the living conditions, the people regularly involved in the child's life and the family life of a child, and even the country where a child is raised. All of this influences the child's development and plays a part in who he or she will become.

While all children develop at a basic rate, there are subtle differences in the time frame from child to child. Some children will progress more quickly through a certain stage and then be a bit behind down the road, and vise versa. However, psychologists and child behaviorists have determined that there are five basic stages of childhood. Knowing and having an understanding of this can help a single mother more adequately address the needs of her children.

Five Stages of Childhood

The five stages of childhood and the ages they are defined as are roughly done so. Different pediatric and childhood specialists categorize the stages with marginal age differentials. Theorists such as Erik Erikson, Jean Piaget, and Lawrence Kohlberg were largely responsible for the defining the following developmental stages of childhood.

Early childhood

Infancy – 0 to 1.5
Toddlerhood – 1.5 to 3
Pre-school – 4 to 5

The most growth changes occur during early childhood than any other developmental stage. Physical development occurs alongside skill development. It is during this time that the greatest language developmental changes will also occur.

Middle childhood

This time period usually lasts from ages 6 through 12. It is during this time that children develop the mindset that they will either be successful or that they begin to doubt their abilities. This is a pivotal time in the creation of a child's feelings of worth.

Adolescence

Adolescence, which is typically used to refer to the time period between the ages of 12 and 18, is largely an exploration of reliance on self. At this stage, a child is truly trying out their competence. Through success, failure, and the reactions of those around them, a child will learn to take risks.

It is often beneficial for the single mother to understand the specific stage her child is at to help her address the feelings and reactions she may encounter when dealing with her child. Instead of feeling overwhelmed by a certain behavior in her child, she will be able to identify it as normal to the place of development her child is in.

Gender Norms

A gender role or gender norm is a set of behaviors traditionally associated with males or females within a social system. Decades ago, gender roles were clearly assigned with males and females being attributed with certain occupations, items of clothing, and styles of behaviors. Today, gender roles have largely blended, in part due to the fact that women have stepped into the workplace and taken on roles that had been traditionally only held by men. With the onslaught of feminism, traditional roles have become less confined.

Men have also contributed to this blending of gender roles. No longer are women the only stay-at-home parents. Today, it is not unheard of for a man to be a stay-at-home father and a child's primary caregiver. As well, men have taken up careers that were once traditionally held only by women. For example, nursing was once a job only held by women, now many men choose to be employed as nurses.

Men and women have more freedom to choose to be and do what interests them as opposed to what society, in the past, has dictated that they should do. The absence of men during war time helped change the roles of men and women, as women took on jobs that only men had previously held. Our culture is largely evolving and gender roles are evolving as well.

The first place a person will begin to develop and experience a definition of a gender role is from his or her parents or the environment in which he or she is raised. Gender roles are not an internal happening; they are developed from outside contributors. Society dictates a large part of what we come to understand as gender roles. For example, television creates an idea in people's minds as to what is expected of a male and a female and advertising paints a picture of what is today's norm for a male or female. This is constantly fluctuating as evidenced in magazines, billboards, and television commercials.

Parents begin at a very early age to instill gender roles within their children, whether they realize it or not, so it is true in assuming that children will look to their parents as role models. By 3 years old, psychologists have found that children have largely developed their gender identity. Gender identity is how a person sees themselves, whether feminine or masculine. A boy will know he is decidedly a boy versus a girl who has already begun to identify herself as a girl. In relating to your children as a single mother, gender makes a difference. While some single mothers say that raising their boys was easier than raising their girls, and vice versa, the reality is it is a different process from one sex to the other, not necessarily an easier one depending on the sex of your child or children.

Raising Sons

Do not be surprised if your son goes through a phase when he expresses a desire to marry you and live with you forever. This normally happens in with younger pre-school and elementary-aged boys. You have been the first woman in his life, and he only has eyes for you. This is entirely normal and commonly happens within both single- and two-parent homes. This is known as the Oedipus complex and will go away when your son experiences his first crush. Oftentimes, this is on an elementary school teacher who he has come to like or a little girl in his class who catches his fancy.

As your son ages, he may become possessive of you. He may feel that when you begin dating his relationship with you is in some way threatened by the new male presence in your life. This is understandable, especially if he is accustomed to being the only male presence in your home. Remind him that you will always love him, as his mother. This topic will be further discussed in this chapter in the section dedicated to dating.

Even though your son will ultimately look to you as his vision of what a woman is, he should not feel or believe that he is the man of the house. He is a child and not an adult. As your son is growing up, it is important for him to remember that it is not his job to take care of you. There is a distinct difference: You are the parent, and he is the child.

Allow your son to rejoice in his maleness. Allow him to indulge in roughhousing and other things that are normally associated with male behavior. If he has an inclination toward sports, instead of discouraging him because you do not know much about the sport that interests him, read up on it. If he is into cars, get him a subscription to a car magazine. When the magazine comes, read it so that you can discuss it with him. Just because you are not a male does not mean you cannot help your son become a man.

Try not to stereotype men because of a negative experience you may have had with your son's father or another man. If you say, "All men are just out for themselves," or make similar blanket statements, you are grouping your son in with the negative qualities you believe men possess. When he hears these statements coming from you, he cannot help but feel some connection to them, as he too is a male.

For a single mother of a boy, the first thing that you should do is learn more about boys — especially if you did not grow up around them. Boys are decidedly different creatures than girls, even at a young age. From a young age, boys like to prove themselves and seem to like the elements of competition where girls have more of tendency to shy away from these things. However, keep in mind, there are girls who will like these decidedly "male" things and boys who will shy away from them. However, this does not mean that something is wrong with your son because he does not thrive on playing a sport like his male cousin does; you should also not be concerned if your daughter has more of an interest in toy cars than in baby dolls.

Try and talk to your son about things you know interest him. If you son favors action movies, take the time to sit down and watch one with him. Doing this will validate him and his interests, and you will be indirectly saying, "I am supporting who you are on the road to becoming." You can direct your son into his manhood even though you are a woman.

Boys tend to be more reticent to share their feelings than a girl of the same age. Again, this is not true of all boys, but it seems to be true for most boys, so be sensitive to this. When your son is at a place where he wants to or is willing to share something with you, create an environment where he can comfortably share his feelings. Be attentive and do not minimize his concerns, however trivial they may seem to you at the time.

Boys need to be given the opportunity to relate to other boys, especially in homes where they are the only male. If he does not learn to relate to other boys, he may begin to feel excluded from things at school and other activities. Boys have a tendency to be more physical than girls do because of the increased testosterone levels they possess. As a single mother, you must set boundaries and limits for your son early on. You must make it known that it is entirely unacceptable for him to be physically violent with you, his sisters if he has them, or any other women in his life. While he may not be bigger than you right now, most likely he will eventually tower over you. With this in mind, it is important to set limits for his actions while he can be physically controlled.

The benefit for a boy being raised by a single mother is that studies show that they will have an easier time relating to a woman in the future. Due to the fact that a boy, raised by a single mother, has more consistent interaction with a woman, he will be more attuned to understanding the female gender as a whole. As well, he will have a greater understanding of a woman's needs than a boy raised by a single father or in a two-parent home. However, this is not to negate the need for male influences and interactions on a continual basis.

Male influence and interaction for a son raised by a single mother is vitally important. Because of the gender differences, the son of a single mother needs to be consistently exposed to male influences.

Keep in mind, your boy is a boy. Because boys have a higher level of testosterone, a healthy boy needs more physical release in a day than a girl of the same age does. Try to encourage your son to participate in some form of physical activity during the day. Whether he takes up running or plays tackle football in the yard with some neighbors, your son needs to be given the opportunity to expend his physical energy. If a boy is not given ample time to release his energy, he will release it in other ways that are less productive and often negative. For example, you may see this reserve of untapped energy leak out in frustration or being quick to get angry.

Make sure you always talk to your son. Encourage him to share what he is experiencing to help become a good communicator. Continuously keep up the communication. When you cannot answer his questions, find someone — particularly another male — who he can talk to. If your son expresses that he has fears about something or that he feels vulnerable, do not lead him to believe that because he is male he should not have these feelings. Instead, listen and hear him out. Then, encourage him in ways that allow him to alleviate his fears or worries. Help him come to an understanding that he can be strong and vulnerable at the same time.

One way to lead your son into understanding that he can be both strong and vulnerable at the same time is to encourage him to do masculine activities while allowing his softness to be protected. Allow him to carry things for you, even if he is young, to let him know his strength can make a difference. For example, when you are carrying in groceries from the car, try giving him something he can carry, and let him know that you appreciated his help. As your son gets older, let him take care of things around the house, even if it is opening a jar of pickles or getting rid of a large spider. Boys relish showing their strength, so allowing your son to assist you will show you value his masculinity. At the same time it is important to encourage your son's vulnerability. Let him know that it is acceptable for him to cry when he loses a favorite pet. Do not embarrass him by sharing the story with others; instead, let him feel safe in showing his emotions. Most of all, when relating to your son, enjoy him for who he is and for who he is on his way to becoming.

Dealing With Daughters

Single mothers do not necessarily have an easier time simply because they are raising a girl instead of those single mothers who are raising sons. There are certain issues that single mothers need to be aware of as they raise a daughter on their own. First, your daughter is not you. Even if she looks very much like you, she is an entirely different person with different wants, needs, and fears. Second, your daughter is not on the same level as you. She should not be privy to adult information simply because you find it is easy to relate to her. She should not become your confidante. This is her time to be a child. Remember that even though she may appear to be mature in her high school years, she has not really fully developed as a woman who is able to handle adult circumstances and issues. Help your daughter develop into a woman you will grow to love not only as a daughter but as a trusted friend.

Compliment your daughter honestly. Children are smarter than we give them credit for, so it is important to give your daughter honest praise, not just what you may think she wants to hear. Encourage her good habits, and gently direct her away from her negative habits. For example, if your daughter tends to gossip and be critical of others, try to steer her away from indulging in these kinds of discussions. Or, if she tends to put herself down, direct her to focus on those things that are positive about her.

Be gentle with offering direction to your daughter and careful when you offer a critical opinion. Oftentimes within a mother-daughter relationship, when a mother points out or criticizes her daughter too harshly, this causes the daughter to rebel or go to extremes. This rebellion is harmful to the daughter and destructive of the mother-daughter relationship.

A weighty subject

Weight can be a very sensitive subject between mothers and daughters. Mothers have to be very careful when addressing their daughters' weight issues, whether they are beginning to add weight or if they have not yet developed and are still maintaining a childish, undeveloped figure. Today's society focuses heavily on a woman's weight, so a mother must combat this with a great amount of sensitivity and caution. Sensitivity is important when approaching this issue with women of all ages, but especially with a teenage girl who is coming into an understanding of her constantly changing and developing body. It is very important to use great tact when broaching the subject of weight with an adolescent and teenage girl.

It must be noted that, while not as common, boys can also struggle with weight issues. They can have anorexia and bulimia and suffer terribly from the effects of each disorder, just as girls can. It is simply not as prevalent. With this in mind, a mother does have to take notice if her son seems to exhibit symptoms, because he is not immune simply because he is male.

On this same subject, it is also important for a mother to watch how and what her daughter is eating. Be aware when your daughter's eating habits abruptly change. Take notice if your daughter is barely touching her food at meals and seems to be pushing it around the plate without consuming any of it. Also, be aware if large portions of food begin to mysteriously disappear from the refrigerator or pantry. Either of these occurrences can be indicative of a girl who is struggling with an eating disorder, whether she is a compulsive overeater or is bingeing and purging. For more information on eating disorders, go to MedlinePlus (**www.nlm.nih.gov/medlineplus/eatingdisorders.html**), a service of the U.S. National Library of Medicine and the National Institutes of Health, or **www.nationaleatingdisorders.org**, a site sponsored by the National Eating Disorders Association. With nearly one out of every 100 hundred students struggling with an eating disorder, it should not be something that is ignored if you suspect that your daughter is exhibiting signs of one.

Before a mother approaches her daughter out of concern she has an eating disorder, it would be advisable to speak to a professional about the situation. Having a discussion with your daughter's pediatrician is a good place to start. You can also bring your daughter in for a physical so that any health risks can be determined before damage is done to her body. By involving a pediatrician, a mother is allowing a professional to evaluate the situation instead of placing the sole responsibility on herself. Dealing with the possibility of an eating disorder with your daughter is a difficult situation for any mother.

As with raising a son, the most important thing a single mother can offer her daughter is open lines of communication. Because you are of the same gender, it may seem that you have more in common with your daughter than you would with your son. If this is true, be sure to take advantage of this and create scenarios where you can begin to develop an open and honest level of communication. If you can talk with your daughter about routine things, for example a show you both watch or a book you both have read, it is easier to transition into more serious subjects when you need to. If you do not talk about the small things, you will have a difficult time discussing more serious issues.

Your daughter will largely learn about life as a woman by watching you. Share not only your successes with her, as proof that she can succeed as a woman, but also let her see your failures and what you have learned from them. As well, let her see that despite your failures, you press on and do not give up.

Sons and Daughters

When dealing with both your children — male and female — it is important is to treat them with equal respect and candor. Do not have a different set of rules for one and not the other simply because they are of a different gender. For example, your son should not be allowed to drive at 16 when your daughter, because she is a girl, is only allowed to drive after she turns 18. Or, your daughter should not be allowed to stay up later simply because she likes the same late night program that you do while your son is told to go to bed because he does not watch the program. The only differences there should be in the rules in your house are differences because of a different in age. For example, the older child will obviously have a later curfew or more household responsibilities than his or her younger sibling.

Your children should be required to treat you with respect, and they should not be permitted to say negative things to you or about you. For younger children, a time-out can be instituted if the child speaks negatively to you or about you. For older children, a mother can simply end the conversation and leave the room, explaining that unless you are being treated with respect, the conversation cannot continue. For a mother to maintain control of the situation, she cannot react in an emotional manner. She must remain calm and control her emotions.

Establishing authority

Your children need to realize that there are boundaries that separate you as an adult and them as children. Failing to establish these boundaries is unhealthy for your child as he or she grows and develops, and it is unhealthy for you as a grown woman. The moment that you become a single mother, you need to begin to establish that you are the parental authority in your home. For some women, this is a difficult task, especially for those who have previously allowed their children's father to discipline and regulate the children's actions, but you can learn to establish authority with your children. If you are creating a new home for your children as the result of the end of a relationship or the death of a spouse, this is a new beginning and you can institute new habits and patterns. Or, if you are starting out with a newborn, now is the time to learn the skills necessary for being the head of a household.

Single Mothers Speak
Kieran Ross, mother of one

"Finding the time to do it all — my homework, their homework, keeping the house together, cooking, cleaning — and not losing my mind in the process is hard. Add in making ends meet, and this makes life close to impossible at times. So, discipline can fall by the wayside at times. This isn't the kids' fault, it's mine. There are times when I don't want to deal with the stress of back talk and the argument that will follow when I tell them what to do; during these times I do what they should be doing for themselves. In the long run, this isn't good for any of us. But, in the moment, it sure seems easier. However, while it may be easier in the moment, I have to get past what would seem to be the quick solution at the time and make the effort to do what is best for my kids, no matter how worn out I may feel. Ultimately, in the long run, this is what is best for all of us."

One way to establish authority is to ensure that everyone is clearly aware of the rules of the household. Once the rules of the household are in place, there must also be consequences in place should those rules be broken. This is a time for you as a mother to offer your children an explanation of how things work and stand firm behind your decisions. Expect your children to not be happy with a new set of rules. Create scenarios that children can adhere to. Also, keep in mind the age appropriateness of the confines you set up. A child not only grows in size but in emotional responsibility as to what he or she can handle. The rules that you set before your children should not have them adhering to an adult lifestyle, but instead, they should have your children behaving in an age appropriate manner.

No matter what rules you set up, healthy children will at some time challenge the rules. Do not be dismayed by this because this in no way reflects bad parenting on your part. However, how you respond to the infraction will determine your success as a parent in this instance. When rules are broken, make it entirely clear that the punishment is a result of a choice the child made to go outside the established rules. Make your child understand that this punishment is their choice because they chose to break the rules. Do not allow this to escalate into an argument. Stay calm, and simply let the facts be known. You are in charge; you are the disciplinarian.

Dare to be a Disciplinarian

There are no bad kids, only kids who are at the time behaving badly. Take heart when your kids behave badly because the cure for bad behavior is consistent discipline.

When a child misbehaves, the first thing a mother should do is let the child know how his or her actions affect her. Do not do this in an overly emotional way, by screaming or yelling. Help your child realize that you understand why they are upset or behaving badly. This is not to say you are condoning their actions; it is instead establishing a report of communication. You are recognizing their feelings, but you are also helping you child understand that his or her reaction to those feelings is unacceptable and will not be tolerated. The earlier this type of interaction can be established, the healthier a relationship you will have with your child. Making your child feel as if he or she is bad is not an effective approach to discipline and will not invoke an improved behavior the next time a similar event occurs.

The goal in disciplining a child is twofold. First, you want to bring about change in future behavior. Second, you want to establish a connection with them and not create a separation. They may not agree with you and your boundaries in the future, but if you have helped them be aware that you understand where they are coming from, you will be leaving the door open for the possibility of better behavior in the future.

Clear and direct communication aids in successful discipline. Explain to your children — before you discipline them — what you expected of them, how they failed to meet these expectations, and then detail the consequences.

Remember that rewarding good behavior is just as important as punishing bad behavior. When your child does something worthy of praise, make sure that you let him or her know you are aware of it. Praise goes farther in creating a behavioral change than criticism does.

Whatever approach you are employing, consistency is vitally important. As a mother and the head of the household, you have to walk a straight line. If something goes wrong one day, discipline should follow; do not let tiredness or frustration get in your way. Take a deep breath, calm your emotions, and apply the disciplinary techniques you have established, even if it is for the 12th time of the day.

Discipline and its tactics need to evolve and change as your children grow and mature. What served as a punishment when they are 6 years old will obviously not serve as an effective reprimand when they are 10 years old. Talk to other parents who are few steps ahead of you to get ideas for punishments that work with their children. Consider their approach, and if you think it would be advantageous, try the technique on your own children. For more discipline ideas and strategies, visit KeepKidsHealthy.com, (**www.keepkidshealthy.com/PARENTING_TIPS/DISCIPLINE/index.html**), a site that offers tips for keeping children healthy. On this website, parents can receive tips for disciplining their children and how to remain level-headed and calm during stressful situations.

With all this said, realize that you are not going to parent perfectly and that is all right because there are no perfect parents. By outward appearances, you may think that some mother is doing it all superbly, but she is not. She is making mistakes with her children, just as you are.

While you are the ultimate authority in the household, you are also the bearer of information, the provider, and the educator. As a single mother, you will wear all these hats and many more. Keep in mind, as you don a hat — whatever that may be — to keep lines of communication between you and your children continuously open.

Let's Talk About Sex

While most public schools across the United States offer sex education as a mandated part of their standard curriculum according to the Guttmacher Institute, in 2002, approximately one third of all teens had not received formal education on the use of contraceptives and one quarter of all sexually active teens had never received abstinence instruction. The reality is, sex education should not only take place at school; it is best to start this lesson at home.

As uncomfortable as this may be for you as a single mother, educating your son or daughter is your responsibility. If the thought of talking about sex with your child leaves you tongue-tied and with a pit in your stomach, prepare yourself. Go to the library or a local bookstore and get some books to read up on the subject. Learn the basics, in real terms. Often when sharing how sex works to a child, it is a good idea to have a few diagrams of the human body on hand. This can make explanation easier as you can forgo fumbling over explanations and refer to a picture of the real thing.

While we all know how sex works, sharing this information with our children can be a daunting task. Glean all the necessary information from whatever resources you choose because this needs to be an ongoing conversation that you will have with your children. While we all may agree that the thought of having this conversation can be overwhelming, a comprehensive place to start is the American Academy of Child & Adolescent Psychiatry website at **www.aacap.org/ cs/root/facts_for_families/talking_to_your_kids_about_sex**. This site helps lead parents through the thought process of preparing to discuss sex and all its ramifications with their children.

If your child brings up the subject, it is obvious they want to know more, and they want to hear it from you. Do not put off their questions; try to answer them to the best of your ability, and if you find yourself stuck for information, make a commitment to get back to them by a specific date and time. This validates that you are taking their interest and obvious concern seriously. Also, it is a good idea to gauge where they are coming from by asking them questions. This will allow you to have an understanding of what information they may have and where they may have gotten that information.

Sex, for a teen, is an awkward subject at best, especially when in a classroom surrounded by their peers. The opportunity to ask questions is often stifled by embarrassment. By providing a foundation of communication on the subject of sex for your teen, he or she will receive a far more healthy and adequate education on the subject.

If you are a single mother of a boy, reach out to the males that you and your son are close to. Allow your son to speak to a man about any questions he may have. These questions can range from, "When will I grow pubic hair?" to "How do I ask a girl out?" While you as a mother may be able to answer each and every one of these questions, there are times when a boy will want to hear these answers from none other than another male. A grandfather, uncle, close family friend, or even your son's pediatrician (if he is male) can offer the answers to your son's questions that only a man can give.

It is completely all right to realize that you, a single mother, cannot do all of this alone. A single mother cannot raise her children entirely on her own. Single or married, the reality is that the old adage is true: It takes a village to raise a child. For your child to become a healthy and thriving adult, you cannot assume that you will be the only role model necessary to shape your child's life. Your child needs more than just you, which is why it is beneficial to supplement your parenting with that a role model to work alongside you.

Role Models

According to the U.S. Department of Health and Human Services, role models in a child's life are vitally important to their development into a healthy and contributing member of society. Children who have role models are more likely to turn to these role models for advice than to turn to their peers. Further, children who have active role models in their life tend to be less likely to engage in fights and destructive behavior than those who do not.

Admittedly, you as your children's primary care giver will be their primary role model. However, it is important to recognize as they grow, develop, and mature, they will look to and need other role models other than just you. Helping them find these role models is an important part of your job as a single mother. If you are a single mother of a daughter, she will first look to you to find the definition of what and who a woman is. She will see how you handle things from house work to relating to men, whether it is the mail man or men you may date. She will gauge her reactions by yours, at least in the beginning.

As your daughter develops, it is important for her to have interactions and relationships with older women other than just yourself. Look to offer her opportunities to relate to women you see as having the attributes you would like to nurture and facilitate in your daughter. This will obviously take cultivating some relationships you might not otherwise have pursued. If you are new to the area or are choosing people you feel your daughter could relate to more than you ever could, this may seem awkward at first. However, you may find that in reaching out for new connections both you and your daughter will ultimately benefit from this.

Find, for example, those women who have attributes you would like to cultivate in your daughter or those traits you see as lacking. Or, if your daughter has developed a certain interest, for example photography, see if you can connect with someone who is an avid or accomplished photographer. Then, ask if it would be all right with them to get together with your daughter. After an initial introduction, allow this relationship to develop naturally. Realize that a role model relationship will never develop if it has to be forced onto your child or if the child is clearly not interested. Think through who would relate best to your son or daughter, not necessarily who you would enjoy the most. The best way to find role models for your children is to get involved in their activities or the things they are interested in. This will give you a clearer vision of the people you might consider as role models for your children.

Another way to present role models to your children is through historically significant males and females. Read up on those with great accomplishments and then introduce them to your children through books, museums, and movies. This will work for both your daughter and your son. You can also introduce role models to your children by getting involved in a service organization. Service organizations offer an opportunity for children to give back and to see adults who are committed to doing the same. Service organizations can range from those who visit the elderly to those who bring sports activities to underprivileged kids. As well, the Boys and Girls Clubs of America offer mentors for children who need them.

If you are a single mother to a son, do not discount the importance you will have as a role model in his life. He will largely learn how to treat and respect women though his relationship with you. However, beyond relating to you, he will need the consistent presence of male role models in his life, especially if his father is not in his life. Boys who do not have active male role models tend to have more anger and higher frustration levels than those who do. They tend to engage in more physically aggressive behavior and have more problems with school established authority, according to psychological findings and the U.S. Department of Health and Human Services.

For those boys who have a father who is active in their lives, it is not as important to seek out male role models for them. However, if a mother feels that her son's father is not providing the kind of guidance and support her son specifically needs, it might be a time to seek out a man who may be able to do this. You might consider seeking out a coach, your son's teacher, or your co-worker.

Boys need gender specific role models. While it may be difficult for a single mother to seek this out for her son, it is imperative that she does so at an early age. By age 3, boys need to relate to other males on an ongoing basis and should not be entirely surrounded by women and girls. By the age of 3, children begin to reason that there are differences in the sexes. Boys need to see active definitions of what masculinity entails, and not just from on television or in the movies.

As a mother, if you do not help your son seek out and establish relationships with healthy role models, your son will seek out men he can emulate on his own, which may not be healthy for him. Oftentimes, the envisioned strength and machismo of a gang member or local bully will appeal to a young boy who is floundering emotionally or feels powerless. Boys will reach to achieve what their role models are achieving, so it is important your son finds a healthy role model. To find positive male role models, consider members of your family, which could be a grandfather, an uncle, or even close family friends. These people will have an ongoing place in your child's life so they can be a consistent presence. Sports coaches often provide a good example, as do male teachers and Boy Scout leaders. Churches and civic organizations often have men who are good roles models for the boys who are involved there. Even a neighbor can prove to be to be ongoing model.

One of the best ways to make sure that any person who your child is relating to as a role model is doing so in a healthy way is to communicate constantly with your child. Additionally, it is important to check in unexpectedly during activities to gage how the relationship is progressing. Constant contact, communication, and involvement can go a great way in forestalling a harmful situation from progressing, should one arise.

When your child initially spends time with someone new, be available or on hand to watch and gauge the situation. Check to see if the person is maintaining healthy boundaries with your child. After your child has spent some time with this person, ask him or her if the person made your child feel comfortable, or if there was anything that he or she did that was off putting or that made your child uncomfortable. Listen carefully for the safety of your child.

When choosing a role model for your son or daughter, it is important to find people who your child can relate to. Children tend to gravitate toward those adults they can relate to, whether they have similar personality traits or common interests. They also want to be near those who they think are successful. A role model should encourage your child to grow and develop as a unique human being. They offer an opportunity for your child to interact with someone older than him or her who is not one of his or her parents.

A role model will also offer support to you. For example, if you are struggling with your child in a specific area, your child's role model may be able to influence your child in a non-threatening way and encourage him or her in a manner that you as a parent may not be able to. Often, children cannot always hear what a parent is telling them, but when they hear the same thing from an outside source, they are more willing to accept this. This is not because of anything you have done as a mother; it is simply an idiosyncrasy for the parent-child relationship.

Admittedly, children need the support system a role model provides. However, single mothers need support systems as well. Support systems for a single mother can come in a variety of different venues, and regardless of what form they come in, they are vitally important for not only surviving as a single mother, but for thriving as a mother.

Chapter 8

Establishing Lifelines — Support Systems

To be a good, healthy, and effective mother you need "Mom Time," which is devoted essentially to you to build up depleted reserves, refocus, and just breathe. You need to have support, whether it is a group of girlfriends or a good therapist. This is not exclusive to single mothers; this is important for all mothers.

> *"So closely interwoven have been our lives, our purposes, and experiences that, separated, we have a feeling of incompleteness — united, such strength of self-assertion that no ordinary obstacles, differences, or dangers ever appear to us insurmountable."*
>
> *— Elizabeth Cady Stanton*
> *Social activist and abolitionist*
> *November 12, 1815 – October 26, 1902*

A single mother cannot simply spend her entire day focused on her children. She needs outlets that stimulate her as an active and vital woman and adult. A single mother cannot depend on teenage children as her support system, no matter how convenient and easy this may appear to be. Your children should be allowed to be children, not to be little adults who you regard as friends or peers.

A single mother cannot think that she will survive on her own. Oftentimes, a single mother may feel that if she asks for help, she is saying that she is not adequate to parent on her own successfully. This is an erroneous statement because no one can possibly ever survive alone. Without adequate support, you and your child will suffer. Do not hesitate to seek out the support you need.

You also must try to focus on the tasks at hand instead of trying to constantly manage the big picture. For example, do not stress yourself by worrying about how you will survive the teen years when your son has not yet reached his first birthday. Or, try not to worry about how you will tell your daughter about getting her period when she is still in diapers. You can survive single motherhood by taking things one step at a time. How you think about your situation will largely dictate how others will respond to the events and occurrences in your life.

Another way that you can begin to support yourself is to recognize where you need help. If you think that you can do this all on your own, you will not make room for someone to support you. Listen carefully to what those closest say to you; if they are telling you that you look as if you need a nap, take the hint. Ask for a reprieve, hand your newborn over to you mother or a neighbor, and sleep for a few hours. Or, if your sister constantly remarks about how your laundry pile never seems to shrink, take the hint and ask for help getting your house organized. Just because you are a single mother does not mean that you can parent singularly. Whether it is someone to watch your kids while you run errands or someone to just listen while your share your thoughts and concerns, no single mother can do it alone.

Support can come from a multitude of places: priests and clergy, family friends, counselors, and even school guidance departments can provide support for not only your children but for you as well.

Another place to begin searching for a support network are the websites on hosted by The Single Mothers network at **www.singlemothers.ca** and **www.singlemothers.org** offered by the National Organization of Single Mothers. These sites not only offer valuable information for single mothers, but they also offer a way to hear other mothers and connect with other single mothers. Forums, blogs, and resources are all included on theses sites.

When starting out without a support system in place, a single mother can feel that she is alone. She may feel that the job of parenting on her own is insurmountable, and this is understandable. The truth is she is not alone. To fully grasp the importance of caring for yourself as a mother, recall the last time you were on a plane. When the flight attendant details what to do in the event of emergency, as a passenger you are always told that you should administer an oxygen mask first to yourself, and then after you have your mask in place, turn and take care of your child. Single parenting is a lot like flying in an emergency; if you are not taking care of yourself, you will most certainly not be able to adequately address the needs of your children.

Mommy Maintenance

Mommy Maintenance is like the regular service your car requires to run well. Mothers of all kinds — not simply single mothers — require time for refueling that should be entirely focused on themselves. This is not a selfish endeavor; it is instead a safety precaution. When a mother is not taking the time to refuel, she cannot withstand problems as they arise, she has less patience with her children, and ultimately, she can become undone.

Mothers Know Best

Florence McGarrity, family counselor, mother of one, grandmother of one

"In respect to the well-being of mother, more specifically a single mother, she needs to be attentive to her own physical, emotional, and spiritual needs. She needs to be as committed to providing these times of refreshment to herself as she is to providing pleasurable times for her children. These times, focused entirely on meeting her own needs, are as important as the care taking and nurturing she does of her children. A mother's mothering will undoubtedly improve as she consistently invests in herself in a healthy and positive way. A mother will be more capable, after re-energizing herself, to cope with the stressors of parenting.

Through my time as a counselor, I have had many mothers say to me that this concept has proved to be a 'lifesaver' for them and for their relationship with their children."

One of the most important lessons a single mother needs to learn is that scheduled Mommy Maintenance is essential. Whether it is a night out with friends or some alone time, every mother needs to unwind without her children at her side. There should be no guilt associated with taking care of yourself. There is a caution label attached to Mommy Maintenance: approach maintenance in moderation. It cannot become an all encompassing force of your focus, and it cannot overtake you so you abandon your responsibilities.

There are two types of maintenance required for every mother to not only survive but to thrive. Mothers need medical and physical maintenance, which means routine check-ups and care when you are physically sick. Also, mothers need to take care of their physical bodies with proper rest, nutrition, and exercise. The second type of maintenance is emotional. This is what keeps every human being feeling alive and cared for and is what keeps each one of us feeling sane and capable. Emotional maintenance consists of those moments devoted to ourselves that refuel our spirits. Keep in mind that most things you recognize as necessary to keep your child healthy should be applied to maintaining a healthy mother as well.

Medical maintenance

As a mother, you are aware of how important it is to keep your children healthy. Whether it is yearly physicals, vaccines, or a trip to the doctor because of an earache or some other childhood ailment, we acknowledge and attend to our child's health care needs because they are vital. However, for many single mothers, that statement seems to only apply to their children and not to themselves. As important as it is to address your child's health care needs, it is imperative to address — and not ignore — your own health care needs.

While a child can see a doctor more than once a month thanks to viral infections and general ailments, a mother will often put off going to the doctor except for yearly routine physicals. When she is under the weather, a mother will often decline going to the doctor, simply because it is a hassle to schedule an appointment and fit it in an already hectic schedule. However, if her child is experiencing the same symptoms she will gladly reorganize her day to get her child the needed treatment.

Women need to have a routine annual gynecological exam and an annual physical. Some gynecologists will perform both exams, while others choose to only conduct the gynecological part so you will need to visit a general practitioner for a complete general wellness physical. Children tend to require more visits to the doctor than adults, but this does not mean that a single mother should forgo going to the doctor for check-ups just because she seems to be "feeling" well. As a single mother, you need to maintain good health for both yourself and for your children so you can continue to be an ongoing part of their lives. Staying healthy requires monitoring.

Choose a physician for yourself in much the same way that you chose a pediatrician for your child. Ask people whose opinions you value to suggest a doctor, and then call and find out if they accept your insurance. Once you have determined the answers to these and a few other basic questions — location, office hours, and the types of services they offer — make an appointment to interview the physician.

After you have chosen a primary care physician, if you are not someone who has been consistent about seeing a doctor regularly, make an appointment for a general physical. This will establish a baseline for the future, and it will also allow you to act preventively should there be anything that is not quite right within your general health.

Rest

Sleep is important to successful mothering. If you are well rested, you handle stress better, you are less emotional, your immune system is stronger, and you have fewer allergies. Sleep regenerates nerve energy, and refuels the liver and the body's cells. Sleep helps replace old cells with new cells, allowing your body to function in a healthier way, a bit like changing your spark plugs on your car gives your car a better start. As well, the body rids itself of more toxins while at rest than it does while in a wakeful state.

According to the Mayo Clinic, people who do not get adequate rest lower their immune systems. They are more likely to get sick, and when they do get sick, they are less likely to recover as quickly as those who are well-rested. Further, the clinic states that the optimal amount of sleep for an adult is seven to eight hours.

Major changes in your life often evoke changes in sleep patterns. For the single mom, this most often leads to decreased sleep rather than too much sleep. With the responsibility of taking care of a child singularly on your shoulders, there may seem to be far less time to sleep than necessary.

Stress in our daily lives can also lead to sleepless nights, as can irregularities in our once ordered schedules. So what is a mother to do? The key to getting enough sleep is to sleep when your children do. As your children have an established bedtime, so should you. Even if you are not tired, begin by getting ready for bed at the same time each evening. Do something relaxing, whether it is listening to soft music or reading a book. Stay away from things that will stimulate you or cause you to dwell on the events of the day. As you begin to be more rested, you will find you are able to accomplish more during the day. While at first it may seem that getting some extra rest is taking time from you, once you are in a healthy, rested state, you will be much more able to accommodate your to-do list.

Nutrition

Along with the need for rest comes the need for proper nutrition. Most mothers have a propensity to think about ensuring their children receive proper nutrients. They hunt down healthy snacks, try to camouflage vegetables in a meal they are preparing, and often encourage their children to have milk instead of soda. Mothers also give their children daily vitamins. But are you giving that same type of attention to your own nutritional needs?

Becoming a single mother is a huge lifestyle change for any woman. Many women note weight changes at this juncture. Substantial weight change that is not intentional is a sign that a woman needs to take some time to truly ascertain what is occurring with her health. No matter how great it may feel to drop 15 pounds without realizing it, it is probably not healthy. Often when a single mother is asked how she has gained or lost ten to 15 pounds, she has no idea. At first thought, she does not realize that her eating habits have really changed all that much. To keep better track of your weight, for a week keep a daily tab of everything you eat. Also, note what time of day you are eating to gain a clear picture of your eating habits.

Often, women will eat or not eat because their life feels out of control. One way to return that state of control is to create a nutritionally balanced plan that includes exercise. Make it a step-by-step process, and do not try to eradicate all your pleasure foods in one fell swoop. Joining a diet program or club can often prove more than a single mother's budget will allow. However, there are hundreds of books that offer general healthy eating plans as well as websites that provide basic plans to follow. These websites offer meal plans, exercise strategies, and even recipes to help you implement a basic diet in your lifestyle.

Downloading new, easy recipes can help. Many websites offer time-effective recipes for creating a meal from beginning to end. Getting in control of your nutrition puts you back in control and will not only boost your confidence at a time when it may be flagging, but the health benefits are undeniable.

Exercise

Exercise is a beneficial way to focus specific time and energy on yourself because it will improve your health and your

figure and is a free way to blow off steam. Another added benefit of exercise is that our bodies release endorphins that act as opiates within the system. Endorphins are what make us feel good after we have exercised.

One thing to keep in mind when starting an exercise regimen is to do so gradually. While exercising can prove to be of great benefit, having yourself so sore the next morning that you cannot get out of bed is not a good thing. Take it slow in the beginning, making slight increases each week. If you are unsure about an exercise program, consult a trainer. Many health and fitness clubs have trainers on staff who are willing to answer general questions.

Mothers Know Best

Casey Weber, personal trainer and mother of two

"It is so good for moms to work out, to get out there and exercise, because let's face it, we all need that extra boost to keep up with our kids. Kids are always active and on the go, and mothers need to develop the strength and endurance to be able to keep up with them. Consistent training helps women accomplish daily tasks with ease.

Being fit will also boost a mom's self esteem. The more in shape a woman gets, the better she feels about herself. Working out allows for positive physical changes to occur within a woman's body, but it also facilitates positive mental changes as well.

When we exercise, the brain releases chemicals in the blood called endorphins. Endorphins cause us to feel less depressed and to have a much greater sense of well being. They also aid in stress relief.

With all that said, one of the best things a single mom can do for herself is to make the time in her schedule to exercise consistently."

Learning to say "no"

Another part of maintaining a healthy balance is learning the art of saying no and not putting yourself on a guilt trip when you do use this two-letter word. The primary reason people have difficulty saying no is because they do not want to disappoint others. Generally, women tend to have more trouble with this than men.

With this in mind, when someone asks something of you, carefully consider the request. Is it something that is easy and requires very little time, or is it something that will require great personal investment? Once you have determined what the request requires of you, decide if you can handle it. If not, be firm in your reasoning. The process begins with convincing yourself how and why the request is not one you should honor. Once you have issued your answer, change the subject. You do not have to offer an explanation; a simple no is enough.

Keep in mind, you are now a single mother with a child whose well-being depends on you. "No" is a necessary and very understandable word to use when the need arises. Not only is it imperative that you need to learn to say no to others, you need to learn the art of saying no to your children. One of the healthiest things you can create for your child is boundaries and limits. When your children are more aware of their boundaries, you as a mother will have a much less stressful time dealing with them. Do not let your children coerce you into permitting them to do things because of guilt. Say no. It is all right for them to not like all the decisions that you are required to make as a mother.

No guilt trips

There is absolutely no time for or benefit to getting caught up in living with guilt about you and your children's circumstances. If you have made a mistake, there is only one thing to do — learn from it and move on. While you may feel your situation is less than ideal, there is no perfect family dynamic, perfect house, or perfect parents. Guilt feeds into the belief system that when you have a problem with your children, your house, or your car, it is in some way associated with the fact that you are a single parent; this is not true. All parents have similar problems.

Differentiating between needs and wants

Learning what you need and what you can handle is an ongoing process, but an important one. You have to determine what it is that your family needs as opposed to what other people are choosing for themselves. While often hard to ignore, the wants must come secondary to the needs.

Needs are things that you cannot do without, including housing, food, clothes and shoes that fit your children, and medical care. Wants, while they may feel like a need, are not necessary for life. A want for a mother could be a new purse that costs $400, and a want for her teenage son could be a pair of sneakers that costs $200. While it is often difficult to say no to the wants, for both ourselves and our children, it is imperative that single mothers learn the art of differentiating between a want and a need.

Bending beats breaking

Bending beats breaking — being able to adjust to your circumstances will prevent you from be broken or overwhelmed by your circumstances or what is happening around you. Being adaptable to circumstances is far superior to being broken by those same circumstances. Changing your schedule or your plans for an afternoon or evening is not admitting defeat; it is being adaptable and making a healthy choice. Give yourself permission to have the option of making a change of plans.

Know that if at the end of the week you are not where you planned to be financially, it is completely acceptable to eat at home instead of going out for dinner. Or, if your children end up home with you for the weekend instead of with their father, plan some fun stay-at-home activities that you would not normally do and choose to enjoy yourself. They key is to look at the turn of events in a positive light instead of a negative one.

You are in control of your feelings and should try and be flexible with how you handle circumstances in your life. You may not be in control of how things turn out, but you are in control of how you react to them. For example, if you have planned a picnic and you wake up to a rainy day, change the forecast for your outing. Instead of giving up on the picnic, have it inside on a blanket in front of the TV and have a movie marathon or a card game bonanza. Or, if you have established a strict bed time of 8 p.m. for your child and you have the opportunity to do something fun and relaxing for both of you, it is important to recognize the opportunity for what it is. Rules are not meant to hinder us from good opportunities that arise; they are simply meant to be guidelines. So when an unexpected event presents itself, bend the rules. Often, giving yourself (and your child) some time off from a set schedule will provide a breath of fresh air when life has become a bit stagnate because of constant pressure.

Maintenance options

It is often a good idea to take some part of the day (even if it is a 15-minute break) for yourself. Granting yourself reprieve of quietness at the start of your day or at its conclusion can prove to be restorative. For some, it is those early moments in the morning before the children are awake when the house is still, quiet, and undisturbed. Whatever fits your schedule, a few moments of "you" time is important. To collect your thoughts, do some deep breathing, read a book, or sit quietly in your favorite part of your home. Doing whatever relaxes you is an invaluable addition to your day.

A long soak in the tub after your children are in bed and asleep can also prove to be a relaxing and cost-free escape. Light some candles, get some bubble bath, put on your favorite music, and indulge yourself. You can also try giving yourself a manicure. A simple softening hand skin scrub, much like you will find in a trendy salon, can be easily made by combining a small portion of salt or sugar with liquid soap or bath gel. Use a coat of your favorite polish to feel pampered without busting your budget when funds are tight.

Even disconnecting the landline or turning the cell phone off for an evening and simply reading a book or watching a movie can prove to be an indulgence because it is time when you do not have to answer to anything but your own agenda. Obviously if your children need to be able to reach you in the event of an emergency, simply screening your calls will have to suffice. But, stick with the screening; do not give in and answer a call that will disrupt your personal time.

There are many more creative — and free — ways to indulge yourself; just think of the things that you really enjoy. If you cannot come up with something fun and cheap to do for yourself, try visiting the website for Wise Bread (**www.wisebread.com/free-and-cheap-fun-things-to-do-in-your-city**). This site offers a list of things to do for $5 or less in your area.

If a night out is really needed but you do not have the money to pay for the evening's activities as well as a babysitter, check into some inexpensive baby-sitting options. Colleges (upon request) will often supply a list of students who have passed rudimentary requirements and are willing to baby-sit for a minimal fee. As well, some students want regular, on-going work and will commit to a weekly pattern of providing child care.

If this is not a viable option for you, see if you can swap baby-sitting services. Check with friends who have children and agree to each watch the other's children for an evening or overnight. Make the evening a special event for your kids and theirs. Making homemade pizzas or ice cream sundaes is fun for all. Prior to the evening, take a survey of what they would like on their fantasy pizza or in a sundae, and then make sure that the ingredients are on hand when the time comes for the kitchen adventure. While you are the baby sitter, laugh and indulge in junk food. Watch a funny, uplifting comedy or play a board game. Then, when the roles are reversed, allow yourself to truly enjoy a kid-free evening. Trust that your children will be well cared for as you are caring for yourself.

Another opportunity for some time for yourself is to get involved in some type of sports activity. Whether it is bowling, softball, rollerblading, or canoeing, being committed to a group activity is a good way to meet people and de-stress at the same time. This packs the added punch of an endorphin surge because of the physical exertion required.

Some mothers find getting together with other mothers a great maintenance tool. Listening to mothers share their stories can give you an understanding to what is occurring in your own home. This is especially helpful if you have children the same age as the other mothers or if they have had a child going through a similar circumstance or issues as your own children. The important thing is to find a connection and support for yourself through a group like this.

While most of these examples will last only a few hours, Mommy Maintenance can run the gamut of overnight trips to kid-free vacations. These options depend on your financial situation and the options you have for long-term child care while you are away from home. A short time away from your children should be a possibility every now and again, as it offers great perspective. Mommy Maintenance is something mothers should do for themselves but never at the cost of the emotional well-being or health of their children. While it takes more creativity to pamper yourself on a strict budget, it most certainly can be done. Whether you spend $5 on nail polish and give yourself a manicure or you indulge in a day at the spa, make sure you leave time to spend on yourself.

Get Out!

When you are a newly single mother — whether you have an infant or recently have found yourself single again — you may feel that you need to focus all of your efforts on your children and parenting them. It can be exhausting, and it can be overwhelming. While it may seem that you should be at home all the time to adequately meet you children's needs, you should not be. You need to get out and socialize. Meet your girlfriends for a cup of coffee. Plan ahead and go for drinks with your co-workers after work. Go to the movies with your mother, or get a spa treatment with your sister. Whatever it is that you enjoyed doing with friends before you became a single mother, you need to set as priority to continue doing now that you are parenting on your own.

While this may seem like a simple concept, single mothers often neglect putting it into practice. It takes some effort to make plans to go out when you have to coordinate your schedule with that of your children's. However, it is well worth a mother's time to refresh herself. She owes it to herself and a mother owes it to her children as well because when she is refreshed, a single mother is a better parent.

The Learning Curve

Another way to offer support to yourself is to learn from others who have already been through what you are experiencing. As being a single mother is largely new to you, seek out those who have been single parents for some time or are single parents of grown children. You will have the opportunity in a group like this to relate to others who know just what you are going though.

Support groups are a good way to connect with other single parents. Parents Without Partners is a viable resource that offers parents and their kids a place to share and learn. This is a national organization that offers local meetings and events. For more information, you can go to its website **www.parentswithoutpartners.org**, which will direct you to local chapters, meeting times, locations, and dates of events.

Parents Without Partners is open to both single fathers and mothers and their children. The group hosts events for parents with their children and separate opportunities for children and parents. Parents Without Partners, and other groups like it, also provides a group environment for your children to naturally become a part of.

Some women prefer an all-women's support group, as opposed to a combined group. Support groups can range from being hosted by a mental health facilitator to sponsored by a church or community center. They can meet weekly or monthly. Some provide child care while others do not. As varied as they are from place to place and group to group, what they offer is quite similar. They are simply a place for a single mother to gather with other single mothers and share insight and experiences. One place to begin your search for the right support group for you is through the website for the National Organization of Single Mothers at **www.single-mothers.org**. This site guides you through finding the group that will best fit your needs. This site also offers a host of other resources every single mother should have at her disposal. You can also find a support group by consulting the phone book and looking on the Internet. If you know of other mothers who attend a group, ask for their advice. Local churches and hospitals often will be able to direct you to groups, as well.

Instant Support

One way to connect with instant support groups is to become involved in your child's activities. By doing this, you will naturally get to know other parents who have children the same age as your children and who are facing many of the same issues you are facing with your son or daughter.

Becoming involved affords you a somewhat candid look at the other parents. You can see how they relate to their children, what discipline techniques they use, how respectful their children are when relating to their parents, and so on. Once you have become comfortable with these other parents, you can begin to seek out their support when you are in need. If you are running late leaving the office, you can ask another parent to pick up your child when they pick up their own. As well, you can reciprocate and offer to drive their children home after an event. This opens up a natural support system with parents like yourself.

"Therapy" for Your Kids

The first thing that you can do for your children as they adjust to all of life's unexpected circumstances is lavish extra affection on them to reinforce that they are truly loved and cared for. This is important, especially during times of change because this type of reassurance reinforces that you are not going anywhere and nothing about your love will change, despite the alterations in their circumstances.

In the midst of changes, do not demand too much from your children as they need time to acclimate and adjust to their new situation. Be ready to listen to where they are and what is going on inside their heads and hearts. Even if you are in the midst of doing something important, when your children want to communicate and share with you, set aside everything else and concentrate on them. By doing this, they will not only feel validated, but it will encourage them to come to you in the future. This also will show them that they are worth listening to. There is nothing more important than letting your child — especially during times of change — know they are valued and their needs are understood. While you may not be able to do anything to change the circumstances they are struggling through, just knowing they have been heard does a lot to relieve a child's worries.

Do not be surprised if your child reverts to old habits or old insecurities. They may pass through these behaviors and revisit certain other behaviors when they are feeling especially unsettled, vulnerable, and fearful due to changes in their circumstances. For example, a child who has always gone to bed easily may resort to saying that he or she is afraid of the dark and does not want you to leave at night. Toddlers may regress from being potty trained to needing to wear a diaper. Elementary school aged children can become overly clingy and apprehensive about attending school, which may be something they had done without hesitation. Or, they may return to sucking their thumbs. This is often indicative that they need reassurance and some extra attention to help them through this time of adjustment. When you acknowledge these needs in your child and address them, you are offering them free therapy from the most important person of their life: you.

For example, if you notice that your child is being extra clingy, make it a point to be extra affectionate and a bit more reassuring. If you are leaving them at school, tell them where you will be waiting for them at the end of the day. In doing this, you are acknowledging how your child is feeling, helping them feel more secure, and in no way minimizing their feelings. Instead, you are validating their needs, which helps them feel more safe and secure.

For example, when your children revert to some habit from their past as a comfort mechanism and you do not tease them or make them feel embarrassed, they feel a bit safer. Do not get angry with them, even if they are reverting to habits that create extra hassles for you. Instead, give them extra attention. If, for example, they are hesitant about going to bed at night, spend some extra time with them. Maybe even use this opportunity of being with your children as time when you can get them to open up and share their feelings with you. This will lead you to be able to help them even more, if you are aware of what is really bothering. Again, it is largely about being available and communicating with your children.

If you are the mother of more than one child, it is important to recognize that the "therapy" you offer one child may not be the "therapy" another child needs. Each child is different and will not respond to the same type of attention. One child may want to sit quietly on your lap and have you brush his or her hair as a comfort, while another child may want to engage in some type of physical activity that requires your attention and involvement. Neither approach of craving your attention is wrong; it is simply different, as are a child's needs and the way that best addresses them.

Listening is Imperative

The only way you are going to be able to gauge what is going on in your children's life is to hear what they are really saying. You cannot address any symptoms they may be exhibiting if you do not know what the real problem is. The only way that you can address the problem is to hear what it is. Give your children the opportunities to talk, and then be ready and willing to listen. Stop what you are doing and look at your child as he or she is talking to you because this shows your child you believe what he or she is saying is important. When you take the time to set aside all else and listen to your child, he or she will feel empowered and encouraged. Your child will feel as if you are on his or her side, even if you do not entirely agree with your child. While he or she is relating what is troubling him or her, never minimize your child's concerns. While these concerns may seem trivial to you, they are not trivial or unimportant to your child.

To help you really hear what your child is saying, try repeating what you think he or she has said and then ask "Is this what you mean?" Give your child the opportunity to correct your interpretation. Once you are both sure that you know and understand what your child is telling you, ask, "What do you think would help?" The answer will afford you added information so that you can move forward in a way that will best help your child. While you may not be able to address or solve a problem in the way your child would most like you to, you may at least be able to incorporate some of their desires within the solution.

Once you have ascertained the problem that is troubling your child, you can establish a support system to help him or her.

Children in Need of Support

Children need emotional and psychological help as much as adults do. A recent study conducted by San Diego University found that there are more high school and college-age students seeking help for mental health issues than ever before. While the cause for this steady incline is unknown, it points to the general need for more support for teens and young adults. About 2.5 percent of all children suffer from depression. Boys under age 10 have a greater tendency toward depression, but by the time girls hit their teen years, the roles reverse and girl have a greater tendency toward depression. However, only 20 percent of those teens who suffer from depression get help. One reason is that while adults tend to recognize their need for help, teens' depression often goes largely undiagnosed or unrecognized. With all the drama in a teen's life, it is often hard for adults to differentiate between normal teen angst and actual depression.

Children and teens in today's world face far greater demands and pressures than those growing up in decades past. Today, the expectations placed on children to succeed are much more demanding than in the past, which creates more stress for children and greater risk for anxiety disorders within younger children. Stress, unfortunately, can lead to depression in some children. With this in mind, it is important to be aware of your children and if they are reaching a place of feeling utterly overwhelmed by their circumstances. These feelings are unhealthy and should be addressed.

As with adults, depression is not a passing bad mood in children, and it is not a condition that will go away on its own if left untreated. Depression can be the result of a number of contributing factors, including change in life circumstances, health issues, hereditary inclination, and environmental contributors.

Some signs that children may exhibit of anxiety or depression can include:

- Mood changes
- Withdrawal
- Changes in sleep patterns – sleeplessness/sleeping all the time (keep in mind that teenagers do have a natural tendency to sleep for long hours. One way to determine if your child is sleeping too much is if he or she is missing activities he or she once thoroughly enjoyed or had a deep desire to participate in)
- Difficulty with concentrating or staying focused on a task
- Unexplained aches and pains
- Extreme irritability
- Overly angry or aggressive behavior
- Crying jags
- Voicing constant negative comments in regard to themselves

These are just a few of the signs that may indicate depression within children. The most important thing for you as a mother to be aware of is changes in your child's behavior. Each child is different, so the way they will exhibit signs of extreme anxiety or depression will largely be unique to them. You are the best determinate in recognizing a problem with your child. If these or similar symptoms or behavior changes are noticeable in your child for more than two weeks, schedule an appointment with his or her pediatrician to make sure that there are no health concerns that are causing these symptoms. If your child's symptomatic behavior is not a physical ailment, consider counseling or therapy for your child. This applies to you as well if you are in need of more help than family and friends can provide.

Unfortunately, for many people the thought of seeing a counselor or psychotherapist is akin to admitting defeat or acknowledging that you are mentally unstable, which is not true. In truth, when you come to terms with the reality that you or child needs help, you are taking a step forward to get help.

Ask your child's pediatrician for a recommendation of a therapist, counselor, or psychiatrist. Consult with any of your family or friends whose children have seen a mental health professional for further recommendations. Other places to check for a list of referral names are your local hospital, a mental health clinic, or a wellness center.

Unfortunately for a single mother, cost often has to be taken into account when searching for therapy options. The first step in the process should be to consult with your health insurance provider. Call them or check their website to see if your insurance covers mental health. If it does, your provider can offer you a list of those people who are in your area and accept your insurance. Many therapists work on a sliding fee scale, which means that you pay the rate that is within your means. Often, you will be required to fill out a questionnaire detailing your household income, and that questionnaire will determine what amount you will be required to pay.

Should your health insurance not cover mental health appointments for you or your child, there are other options such as Medicaid-provided assistance or non-profit programs. Many school systems also offer a school psychiatrist who will work with your child, especially if his or her issues are affecting his or her performance in school. Contacting the school nurse or the school guidance department will provide you with the policy governing where your child attends school.

If you do go forward making an appointment for your child — or yourself — realize that establishing a relationship with a counselor, therapist, or psychiatrist is a lot like becoming friends with someone new. If you do not feel comfortable with the person or your child feels that he or she cannot talk with the person comfortably, seek out someone who your child can feel at ease with. Feeling safe and secure with the person will largely affect the progress that is made during the sessions.

An initial counseling or therapy session is a time when you and/or your child will be required to fill in a large amount of background information so that the professional you are seeing can get an understanding of the best way to help you and also to most accurately determine what your needs really are. Be willing to tell your story. Be honest and reveal the details and events that led up to the appointment; the more information you can provide, the more the therapy sessions will help. Keep in mind the therapist or counselor may recommend that you come in for a session or two or for a part of your child's sessions so that you and your child can work together on whatever issues he or she is struggling with.

Another option, for you and for your child, is family counseling. This is group therapy where you all work together to facilitate a healthier situation and outcome. This is especially effective for establishing an ongoing supportive environment within the home. Oftentimes, if your child's father is an active participant in your child's life, it is a wise idea to include him on some of the sessions so the two of you can work as a team to restore a sense of equanimity in your child's life.

The number of visits you and/or your child will make to a therapist will depend on the issues that need to be addressed; there is no magic formula. Some issues require more time to deal with than other issues. The average time for treatment is six months, but this does not mean that if you continue after six months, you have more serious problems. Instead, it is indicative that you need a longer time of ongoing help and support.

While knowing that you have a list of people you can call in the event of an emergency can help, sometimes single parenting and living in a house as a single adult can be very isolating and lonely. While other mothers seem to thrive in this new setting on their own, some mothers desire to have a partner.

Two are Sometimes Better Than One

Some single mothers believe co-habitating with another single mother and her children is an optimum experience. Co-habitating offers the opportunity for two single mothers to share one home. Instead of having to shoulder the burden of a house or apartment on their own, two mothers choose to live together to reduce the financial burden. The dynamics of how this shared living space works out is unique to each situation.

Not only does this type of co-habitating offer ongoing support, it dramatically reduces expenses for both families involved. By pooling resources, sharing a home, and no longer living alone, some single mothers find that co-habitating is not only beneficial to them but a good opportunity for their children. Often, mothers find that they initially choose to co-habitate due to economic reasons, but as time progresses, the real support they receive is emotional. Having another mother as a back-up system when they cannot get home on time for work, or when they are ill and need a bit of help, is far more important to them than the money they are saving by sharing a home.

Each living dynamic is different. Some mothers choose to pool everything, from resources to food to their children sharing bedrooms, while other mothers choose to simply share a house but to live more separate lives. The choice is entirely up to the two mothers who commit to sharing a residence.

CoAbode Single Mothers House Sharing is an organization designed to connect women who are looking for housing partners. The organization allows you to search for mothers in your area looking to share a home or apartment. While the basic premise of the group is to help women establish connections for co-habitation, the group also offers access to other single mothers and directs you to resources that are available in your area. Their foundational premise is that two single moms raising children together can achieve more than one struggling alone. Their website, **www.co-abode.com**, offers a nationwide avenue for connection.

Another option to look into when considering co-habitating is the Neighborhood Assistance Corporation of America (NACA), which is a non-profit advocacy and housing assistance organization that helps low- to moderately low-income families obtain a mortgage with little or no down payment. They also help those at risk for losing their homes due to difficulties in maintaining consistent mortgage payments refinance and lower their monthly payments.

Playmates

As much as you may need the support of another mother, your child needs the support of his or her peers. As your life changes, especially if you and your children have navigated a divorce or suffered the loss of their father, children need to remain connected to peers.

If you have recently relocated, make every effort to find activities that your child can become involved in. A good place to start is to request information at the school your child attends on any age-appropriate activities offered in your area. Another place to check is the local town hall or recreation center. Asking the parents of your child's classmates often provides a good resource, as they may have children who are already participating in a specific activity or can direct you to activities that you may not have yet considered for your child. Another way to find companions for your children is to choose something that they may have especially felt comfortable doing where you used to live because this will naturally open up the potential for friendships to grow. Allowing children to meet naturally is far more comfortable than two parents creating a scenario for their children to meet.

Make every effort to be willing to taxi your child here and there in the beginning because this way he or she will have the opportunity to become part of a group. Do not discount the importance of these connections. As you and your children are on your way to forming connections, you are also on the road to mapping out a new community that is uniquely your own.

One of the ways you may be considering expanding your community is by entering the dating world. Emerging as a single mother in the dating world is something that takes some careful thought but can lead to great new and unexpected adventures and even romance.

Chapter 9

Leaving the Old Maid At Home —
Entering the World of Dating

Dating and All Its Dilemmas

> "She's got most of the symptoms – is twittery, and cross, doesn't eat, lies awake, and mopes in corners."
>
> – Louisa May Alcott (from Little Women, on dating/being in love)
> American writer
> November 29, 1832 – March 6, 1888

For single mothers, the choice to start dating can be a complicated one. Some mothers are struggling through feelings associated with the death of a spouse or residual anger from a divorce while other single mothers may simply have put off dating to focus on the responsibilities of being a single mother.

Single Mothers Speak

Kieran Ross, mother of two

"Dating is like a second job and is hard for anyone, but it is really hard with young children! I find the biggest challenge is finding the time to date. The other major challenge is that when I was single, I expected certain things from the men I went out with, but now that I am a mother, I expect and want a whole lot more. Now, as a mother, I am extra careful and extra picky when choosing anyone that I would consider going out with."

Whatever your circumstances, dating as a single mother will prove to be a formidable experience. For the first time, you now have to consider how dating will affect not just your life, but how it will affect your child's life. You are no longer just single; you are a single mother. The people you choose to date have the potential of becoming an ongoing presence in your life as well as the lives of your children.

Before you set out to start dating again, take a personal inventory of yourself. See if you are really content and fulfilled on your own. Ask yourself if you are at an emotionally healthy place. If you have someone who you are especially close to and can trust, ask him or her if he or she thinks you are ready to begin dating again. Remember that a romantic relationship should add to you; it should not be something that you are seeking out because you are not strong enough to stand on your own. You need to be in a place where you are content and fulfilled on your own before you seek out the romantic company of another person.

Another important factor to take into consideration when contemplating the concept of entering the dating world as a single mother is whether you are pursuing dating because you want a relationship or because you simply desire companionship. Desiring physical closeness with another human being is natural. It is important to evaluate if what you really want is simply intimacy with another person or if you are at a place where you desire the commitment and the work required to maintain a relationship. There is nothing wrong with desiring companionship versus wanting a relationship; you just need to make sure you recognize where you are before you put yourself out in the dating world.

Single Mothers Speak

Helena Grant, mother of three

"Very soon after my first marriage ended, I got involved with a man. I didn't want to be single, and I did not want to be alone. I wanted to be taken care of. We started dating and quickly got serious. At the time, being with someone — anyone — seemed like the perfect solution to my loneliness. The relationship was not a good one, but I stayed in it because he took care of me and my kids. It took me a while, but I finally did see that this was not a good situation for me or my kids.

> *It was hard for me, but I made my way out of that harmful relationship. It was not good just to be with a man because I was lonely, and I would tell any woman in the same situation that this is not the right reason to be involved with a man."*

A relationship will not make a single mother feel fulfilled if is she lacking or is recognizably unfulfilled in her life as it currently is playing out. Oftentimes, women believe the fairy tale that a relationship will lead them to a happily ever after ending in life. Many women believe that if they simply find a man, their issues and problems will be solved: They will no longer feel insecure, emotionally lacking, or spiritually depleted if they have a partner. However, this is not the case.

The key to understanding where you are emotionally is to ask yourself the following questions:

- Do I want to get something from the person I will potentially be involved with, or do I envision myself bringing something to a relationship?

- Am I looking for a relationship simply to fill something missing in me?

- Am I at a place where I can be a contributor in a relationship, or will I only take from one?

It is unhealthy to expect to become more than you are because you are now in a relationship. Wanting to be a part of a relationship, sharing your attributes, and contributing to a relationship is healthy.

As a woman, when you are not in an emotionally healthy or good place, you will attract people who will meet your needs in unhealthy ways. For example, if you are feeling a lack of confidence and feel as if you need to be taken care of, you may attract someone who is controlling in an unhealthy way. As a mother, this will create an unhealthy scenario for your children. As your children's primary role model, you do not want to involve them in an unhealthy situation that at some later date they may misguidedly emulate. With this in mind, avoid rebound dating. If you are newly single, allow yourself time to grieve, grow, and acclimate to your new life as a single mother. While this time of singleness is very important for your emotional health, it is just as important for the emotional health of your child as well. Give yourself time to transition into your new life before adding another component to adjust to.

The important thing to keep in mind is that absolutely no one but you can determine when you are ready to begin dating. Many people have ideas about your need to date, but the only person who knows when the correct time arrives is you. Listen to others, and then decide for yourself when you are ready. Then, take a few logical steps to prepare yourself for this new life adventure.

If you feel confident that you are at a place that you are emotionally healthy and satisfied on your own, and you would like to pursue a romantic relationship, consider defining what your ideal mate would be like. Ask yourself a number of questions. The following are a few suggestions:

- What am I really looking for in a partner? Making an inventory of what qualities you do and do not want in a partner will help you decide ahead of time what is or is not acceptable.

- Would I be interested in a single father? Keep in mind if you get serious with a man with children, you will have to incorporate your child's needs and his children's needs.

- Am I comfortable with someone who drinks and/or smokes?

- Would I be interested in a long-distance relationship, should the opportunity arise?

- How am I going to coordinate my schedule to include dating?

- Can I afford a baby sitter?

- Do I feel comfortable dating people who are involved with my children (coaches, teachers, etc.)?

These are a few questions that will help you define what you are looking for in a partner. It is important to know what attributes would make you happiest. You need to be aware of these things before you become involved with someone, not after, because after you become involved with someone, it is often difficult to see clearly what you really want.

Somewhere Out There

Now that you have decided that you are ready, willing, and mentally able to handle dating, the next question often becomes, "How do I find a date?" Often single mothers find that the easiest place to find a potential date is right where they are. Attending their children's activities, grocery shopping, running errands, and living out their daily lives affords some single mothers a plethora of opportunities to meet potential dates. However, some single mothers make the choice that they would like to maintain some distance between their lives as mothers and their lives as dating women. They decide that they do not want to date someone who is connected to their child, whether it is through their child's activities or perhaps another child's parent. They feel that they do not want to risk the uncomfortable feeling that can arise when a relationship sours. This is understandable. However, making this decision can make meeting someone new a bit more difficult.

One way to meet new people is to get involved in an activity that genuinely interests you. If you have an interest in hiking, join a hiking group; if you like chess, try attending a chess club meeting. By choosing an activity that genuinely interests you, you have at least that initial interest in common with the people you will meet. Further, if you do not make a romantic connection, you will at least have enlarged your circle of acquaintances, and this often may afford you the opportunity to meet someone by way of a mutual connection.

Charity work is another place to meet like-minded people. If you are willing to invest yourself in giving to others, performing charity work is an easy way to meet people with the same values. Churches and houses of worship oftentimes will host events for singles or adults in the same age group. This affords those people who choose to attend church or religious services a faith-based way to meet others of the same belief system. Many single mothers find these groups and groups like them a good starting pint for meeting potential dates.

Matchmaking services and websites designed to connect singles have become very popular venues to meet like-minded people. Often, these services come with a price tag ranging anywhere from $5 a month for some sites to thousands of dollars for professional matchmakers. One of the most important precautions a single mother should take when registering with a website is to ensure that personal information — like your home address and phone number — are not disseminated throughout the site. Most sites today ensure the safety of their users. To ensure this does not happen, it is important to read all the fine print before registering for a site and supplying personal information.

Two popular online dating sites you can purchase a membership to are eHarmony (**www.eharmony.com**) and Match.com (**www.match.com**). Each of these sites allows members the opportunity to create a profile and peruse other members' profiles. These sites allow the member to control the amount of contact they have with other members of the site.

Butterflies and Sweaty Palms

For some single mothers, stepping into the dating world brings a rush of anticipation and excitement. For others, the idea of entering the dating world brings feelings akin to panic. Either reaction is not abnormal as dating and meeting someone new brings with it a host of new emotions and a small sense of fear for those women who have been hurt in the past.

If you are a mom who has long been single and has spent a great deal of time with your child, their friends, and other parents, you may wonder what you will possibly bring to the table as you sit down to dinner on your first date. You may wonder if you will have anything interesting to say. You may even ask yourself, "Will I be able to contribute to a conversation without discussing Thomas the Tank Engine or Big Bird?" These feelings and fears are understandable. All people who are dating feel similar apprehensions when spending time with someone new. These feelings are not unique to a single mother. However, there is an easy remedy when you are unsure about what to talk about: Get your date talking. Everyone likes to talk about themselves and the things that interest him or her. There is no more effective tool to start a conversation than to start asking your date questions. Questions can include:

- What do you do for a living?
- How many siblings do you have?
- What do you like to do in your free time?
- Do you like sports? What is your favorite sports team?
- What is your favorite vacation spot?
- Do you like to travel? Where have been?
- What kind of food do you like? Do you like to cook?

Be prepared to be an active listener. Do not let your date feel that you have tuned them out and that you are simply letting them go on and on. If you do not know about something they are sharing with you, ask your date questions. You may find that you do not want to go out on another date with the person, but you may have learned something new.

As for you, just be yourself. If you like something, let your date know. If your date asks for your opinion or asks you about your likes or dislikes, be honest. Keep in mind, this may be someone who you see again, and you do not want to feel that you have presented yourself in a less than honest light down the road.

Most importantly, keep in mind that your date does not want or need to hear your tales of woe on a first or even second date. On a date, a person is not there to listen to rotten tales of how horrible your former husband was or continues to be. Reserve those stories for your girlfriends who will gladly give you a lending ear. Some topics you want to steer clear of on a first date include politics, finances, and your past relationships. While these topics will come up naturally during your courtship, there is no need to let your date know everything about you all at once.

If during the course of a date, you realize the person you are with is not aware that you are a single mother, the best thing to do is to allow the subject to come up naturally. For example, if the topic of weekend activities comes up, naturally including the fact that you attend your son's baseball games on Saturdays is an easy way to introduce the fact that you have children. Or, if the question arises of what a typical night after work includes, a light answer detailing the craziness of your household at dinner can easily make a date aware that your household consists of more than just you.

The Big Decision —
The Big Revelation

Once you have decided to begin dating, the first person that you should tell about your decision is your child. Honesty is important, and you need to help them understand that just as they have friends and relationships, so will you. While you are sharing the facts with them, keep the information to a minimum. You can begin by sharing that you would like to start dating, and a good time to do this may be before you even have your first date a single mother. By doing this, once you have met someone you plan to go out with, let your children know that you will be going on a date. Allow them to ask questions if they are interested, but do not feel hurt if they initially seem uninterested in your date.

Give them prior warning as to when a date will be coming to the house to take you out for an evening. Having a new person show up at the door and whisk their mother away for an afternoon or evening out can be unsettling for a child and cause your child to feel worry and resentment. It is a good idea to make a simple introduction and let your children know where you are going and what time you expect to return. This gives them a sense of being a part of this new aspect of your life instead of being shut out of it.

Boys will sometimes have a greater degree of adjustment when their mom begins dating. This stems from a boy feeling he is the man of the house, and when his mother begins dating, he can feel his role is being usurped. His jealousy stems from the reality that he has not had to share your affection with anyone else. This is normal; however, it should not be reinforced. As his mother, you should remind him that the love you have for him is different from any feelings you may share with the person you may be dating. That love, a mother's love, is not something that will ever come to an end or change.

For this reason, and others, it is not a good idea to instantly make your new love interest a part of you and your children's life. Take some time. If this person is as wonderful as you believe that he is, he will be willing to take things slowly for the good of you and your children. Get to know this person first before introducing him to your children. See what he is like in a number of different settings. For example, spend time with your friends and see how he reacts to them. Then, spend time with his friends and notice how he relates to them as well. Before risking your children growing attached, see if you can form an attachment of your own with this new person.

One of the best ways to tell if the person you are involved with is someone you want around your children on an ongoing basis is to ask yourself, "Is this someone I would like my children to grow up to be like?" If you cannot answer with a resounding yes, it may be time to reconsider the direction your relationship is headed.

Who is This Person?

Ask yourself some questions about the person you are dating, including whether this a person who you feel safe and comfortable with. Is this a person who encourages you to be yourself, or is this a person who wants you to make changes in yourself? If a person you are dating wants to initially change you and you have barely spent any time together, this should be a warning sign to you that the relationship is headed in an unhealthy direction. If the person you are dating has a genuine interest in hearing about your children, this is a good sign. If he seems bored, disinterested, or ignores the topic of your children, you should take this as a sign that your children may become an issue if you two are to continue dating.

Listen to the things the person you are dating is saying. If he tells you that he has children he never sees, take this into consideration when thinking about a future with him. If he is not involved and has no relationship with his own children, how then will he relate to yours? If he maligns his ex or speaks in derogatory terms, listen to what he is saying. His words may be sending you a message of how he treats the women in his life. If he speaks ill of her, he will most probably be on a pre-set course to treat you in a similar manner. Unfortunately, it is even easier the second time around to treat a person poorly. If he cheated on his first wife, the likelihood is that he will do it again in another marriage relationship. This is not a steadfast rule, but it seems to happen more likely than not. While this is not true of every man, it should serve as a cautionary yellow light. Simply let it make you a bit more careful of the way your relationship progresses.

Take stock of your dating relationships in a logical, non-emotional way. One of the ways to reduce your emotions when evaluating a relationship is to write down the pros and cons of the relationship. Then, put the list away for a week; do not look at it or read it over during this time. After the week is up, take a look at the list and you will be afforded a less emotionally driven response to the items on the list. If you are honest with yourself about making the list and then taking it to heart, you will be able to evaluate where you are more effectively. This will lead to healthier relationships in the future.

Once you have seen enough of this person to really know that you are interested and would like to take your relationship to the next step, gradually include them in activities with your children. However, always confirm with your children first that they are comfortable with this. For example, if you have a son who plays football, do not invite this new person to your son's game without checking to see if your son is comfortable with this arrangement prior to the person just showing up. Or, if your daughter is performing in the school musical, ask her if it would be all right with her if you brought a date. These two examples are quite general; however, they point to a level of respect that is important to offer your children.

However, if you are inviting the person over for a meal, inform your children that your significant other will be joining you and let them know before the doorbell rings. Or, choose a neutral location for a first group activity you will invite your new partner to. For example, go to an amusement park or an arcade where the focus is off of you and this new person and the focus is instead directed toward the activity.

Once you start dating, it is important to be sensitive to how your children react. Some children may get concerned that if you have a significant other you will leave them or that you will not pay attention to them. Reassure them that this is not the truth and that the feelings you have for this other person are not the same type of feelings that mothers have for their children. Schedule "dates" with your children; whether you go out or stay at home and just talk, let them see that just because you are involved with someone new does not mean that you do not have time to spend with them. During these "date" times, let them see that the time you spend with them is special, set aside, and devoted just to them and for them. Remember they may also feel threatened that this new person will take you away from them. If you sense this in your children, if they are old enough, talk to them about their feelings. Regardless of their age, provide constant reassurance that you are not leaving them despite the new relationship you are in.

Expect the unexpected

While telling your children that they will soon be meeting the person you are dating may go much better than you anticipated, be ready to expect the unexpected. When under pressure, children often elicit behavior that is entirely out of character. This can be due to nerves, jealously, or a host of other emotions. When your date initially meets your children and you feel that they have behaved abominably, or you are so thoroughly embarrassed that you feel you might want to consider the witness protection program, simply explain that children do the darnedest things. If their behavior is entirely unacceptable, excuse yourself and your children and handle the matter in private.

Do not reprimand your child in front of your date. If his or her actions require immediate attention, take your child to another room and discipline him or her there. Then, explain that you realize that he or she may not be happy or comfortable with this new situation and this new person, but acting out is not acceptable and will not be tolerated. Set boundaries for your children. If you make it clear to your children early in your relationship that you expect them to behave with decency, it will be much easier for them to adapt. Remember, children crave structure and boundaries. By establishing boundaries, you will be offering them these important elements

Introductions all around

If you are in a relationship with someone who has children from a previous relationship, this adds another element into first introductions. Oftentimes, it is easiest for your significant other to meet your children first before introducing the two groups of children to one another. This way your children will receive undivided attention, and you can then do the same for his children. Get to know each other's children before adding both sets of children into the mix. Spend time with them so you have a feeling for their personalities and so they know who you are.

Admittedly, the best scenario, the one you all are hoping for, is for all the children to like each other and get along. However, this may not happen at first. Let your children know that while you hope they like your significant other's children, it is all right if they do not. Your only requirement of them should be that they act civilly to the other children.

Scheduling activities that require physical activity will help the transition of spending time as a group go more smoothly. Plan a hiking trip, an afternoon spent ice skating, or a trip to an interactive museum or amusement park. By offering the children something to do while they are all together, the pressure to relate to each other will decrease. Instead of focusing directly on making conversation or getting to know each other, they will be focusing on the activity and relating indirectly to each other.

Limit the time that you spend together as a group initially. If things are not going well, having shorter interactions will be more manageable. If things are going well and everyone is enjoying each other and getting along, you will leave each other on a positive note and with the desire to be together again. As a mother, you know that children are like fresh produce and they have expiration dates. When you allow them to stay up too late or play too long, they get in rotten moods and behave in ways that are less than pleasant.

Children need time and patience to develop relationships, so do not be despondent if everything does not go well the first few times you all are together. Instead, give everyone time, space, and opportunities to get to know each other.

PDA

Public displays of affection, also known as PDA, can make children feel left out and uncomfortable. Try to keep intimate moments of kissing and snuggling to be just that: intimate. Reserve these moments for those times when you and your significant other are alone. While it may feel wonderful to spontaneously engage in a long kiss, the likelihood is that this will be anything but wonderful to your children.

While having your new partner spend the night might prove to be a great temptation, do not succumb. This is a very cumbersome and weighty subject for children to deal with, especially if their father is still an active and ongoing part of their lives. Keep in mind that a former spouse can use this information against you in legal proceedings and if custody agreements are revisited.

The time frame in which your relationship progresses is entirely up to you. However, as a single mother, you will need to be guided by your feelings as well as the feelings and emotions of what is ultimately healthiest for your children. Think through your decisions and remember that your choices will set a precedent for how your children will act in the future.

As a single mother, these choices of how to progress in a relationship and how to introduce a new person into your life and your children's lives are largely circumstantial; there is no formula. You have to be attuned to what is best for your children, and you have to be willing to put your needs and desires on the back burner if your feelings contradict what is best for your children.

While you are going through the dating process, keep in mind that you are an example. The way that you and the people you date interact serves as the model that your children will begin to follow when they consider dating. Keep in mind if you would not consider the person you are dating as a potential role model for your children, you have made a wrong choice about who you are dating.

While being involved in a romantic relationship can create a future for a single mother, she should not depend on a partner for that. A single mother has the future before her, and while she may feel overwhelmed by her current circumstances, with a bit of strategizing, careful planning, and a dose of hard work she can have the dreams she envisions come true.

Chapter 10

Somewhere Over the Rainbow — The Future

Admittedly, being a single mother is not devoid of challenges. You are the one who your children depend on; you are the one they look to for support, advice, and direction. Ultimately, you are the one their future begins with. The future is a winding road before you — and your children — so where are you headed down that road?

> "It's not only children who grow. Parents do too. As much as we watch to see what our children do with their lives, they are watching us to see what we do with ours."
>
> – Joyce Maynard
> American writer
> November 5, 1953 -

Being a single mother is not so much about the route you took to becoming a single mother — whether it was by choice, by divorce, by the death of a spouse, or any other scenario for that matter. Being a single mother most importantly is about the road you are now headed down and where you expect to find yourself along that road over the next months and years. No matter how you feel about the place you find yourself in at this very moment, whether you really like it or find that you wish your circumstances were different, you have choices and opportunities. Even if you are completely satisfied with your current circumstances, it is imperative that you have goals.

The future starts right here, right now with you. It will not start with things happening around you. The future — your

future — will start inside of you. The future is all about living out the belief that you can have what you want, be whom you want to be, and achieve your dreams. If you are not willing to take a chance on your dreams, no one else will. Your success depends on you and your willingness to persevere. Success is largely determined by how hard a person works. Success is a mindset, and a single mother needs to have a mindset of success to achieve her dreams.

Planning Your Success

One of the most promising things that a single mother can do for herself is to look forward to her future. Being a single mom does not mean you need look to the future with fear and trepidation. Single motherhood does not have to be the curse that some make it out to be; it offers great future for both mom and kids. You get to decide what the future holds, so start planning.

The first step in making a plan for the future is deciding what it is that you want your future to be. Here are some areas you may want to take into consideration when creating your vision:

- Family: What do you desire for your future as a family? What do you want for your children? What goals do you have for their future that you need to start planning for now? Do you need to start saving for private school or planning for college?

- Financial: What changes would you like to make financially? Would you like or need to be to be making a larger salary?

- Career

- Attitude

- Health/well being

- Philanthropic

- Indulgences

Establishing Goals

To start you on your way to achieving your desires, make one goal you can accomplish today. Make it simple. For example, it could be making a call to get a college catalog listing the next semester's classes or making an appointment to get your hair freshly styled. Whatever you choose, do it. Take that first step.

Once you have accomplished that goal, make a list of approximately ten things that you would like to have six months from now or even a year or ten years from now, depending on how far ahead you would like to begin planning. This can include taking the steps to return to school, checking out other career opportunities, joining a gym, losing ten pounds, getting involved in an organization that interests you, or even going on vacation. Do not let anyone choose the items on your list but you.

Then, after you have made a vision for your short-term future, begin a similar list for your long-term future. Make a list of what you would like to do and where you would like to be five years from today. Be descriptive, create pictures in your mind, and get them down on paper. The more you can envision, the more likely your success will be. Take time to think through your list. Give yourself a week to create this long-term list. Really afford yourself the opportunity to think through the items.

If you need a helping hand in getting started or some direction for different types of goals, you may want to consider visiting myGoals.com (**http://mygoals.com**). This site has goal-setting software and templates that can serve as a directive to getting started creating goals. This site will even send reminders to help you stay on track and at the level of achievement that you have mapped out for yourself.

The way you set goals is paramount to the amount of success you will achieve. Goals need to be specific and concrete, and they need to be divided into manageable size pieces.

Set goals that are SMART:
  S - specific
  M – measurable
  A - achievable
  R - relevant
  T – timely

Reaching your goals

In regard to goal setting, the long-term goals are much more important than you may at first realize. The long-term goals, while lofty and far down the road, will determine your short-term, day-to-day living. To accomplish your goals, you have to be proactive and start planning for your future. First, begin with the attitude that you will never take no for an answer in regard to the items on your list. No matter your present circumstances, you have the opportunity to change them. Keep this in the forefront of your mind as you take the next steps in planning your future.

Next, write out a descriptive paragraph about each item on your list of goals. This will remove any vague ideas and help make your vision much more clear. While this step may appear unimportant, it is not. Having a clear and defined vision is vital to obtaining success. By knowing exactly — not vaguely — what your vision is, you will be more able to concentrate your efforts. You cannot focus your efforts on something ill defined or something you yourself cannot see.

After you have written out the descriptions, look at each item separately. Make a list of what it will take to accomplish each item. Be detailed. If you have to purchase an item that costs $5, put it on the list if it is necessary for you to achieve your goal. There is a two-fold purpose in creating these kinds of structured and outlined goals for yourself: First, it allows you to have every detail taken care of so you will have a far greater opportunity for success. Second, the more short-term goals that you achieve, the more accomplished you will feel. Feeling that you have accomplished a prescribed regimen will encourage you to take the next necessary step to achieving a goal.

For example, if your goal is to take a vacation with your children a year from now, one of the first smaller goals would be to decide where to go. To do this, you would need to gather information on a number of destinations before ultimately deciding where you want to go. Then, you would need to take the steps to begin saving the money required to pay for all the activities on your vacation. Opening a savings account for this specific goal might be a good idea, and it also represents a goal that is necessary and easy to achieve. A smaller goal could be to peruse the sale racks at the end of the summer season for new clothes and shoes you and your children will need on your vacation. All these are examples of a series of smaller goals that you will need to achieve prior to embarking on your vacation. If you plan well and accomplish your goals, your vacation will be everything you dreamed it could be.

Conquering Doubt

Realize that along the way — for both your short-term and long-term lists — there will be times or even days that you feel hopeless and that your dreams and goals for the future are unattainable. This is a normal part of life. When you start to feel overwhelmed, it is a great time to take out your list of goals and recount for yourself each of the goals you have met to date. This serves as an analysis of what you are able to do. Analyzing goals you have previously met also serves as a reminder of why you should not give up. You have come this far and are part way there already. You have been moving forward; your small goals are a testament to that.

For a single mother, the most important part of planning a future is to realize that you have options; you are not trapped in. However, stepping out and going after your heart's desires requires taking risks, which can be scary — especially for a single mother who has children. Every small goal you achieve makes success more tangible. The more you succeed in the small things, the less scary taking bigger risks will become.

Preparing for the Future

As mothers, one of the most common mantras you will repeat for school-aged children most certainly is "Do you homework." When setting goals and planning for the future, one of the most important things you can each do to ensure the success of any venture is to learn all there is to about the goal you have set.

If you want to open your own business, for example, learn everything there is to know about that business and its costumers. Do not be afraid to ask questions from professionals and those who work in the business you are interested in. Network and begin to build relationships with people that you can maintain. Careful research — homework — will lead to preparedness and ultimately to success. No matter what you are planning for the future, whether you want to start a business, buy a home, or plan for a return to school, do not leave the necessary homework incomplete.

Flee From Negative Thinking

Once you have your plan in place and your homework is complete, resist the temptation to second guess yourself or to question if you have what it takes to reach your goals. Your thought process will be your greatest deterrent to success.

If you believe that you cannot achieve success, the reality is that you probably will not. Those people who begin by believing in themselves play a large part in others believing in them. For example, the exuberant woman who goes in to apply for a small business loan and who presents a well-researched business plan for her small bakery is far more likely to get approved for the loan than the woman who goes in and says that she is really not sure whether her idea will work and shows the loan officer a hand-written proposal on a page of loose leaf paper. Your attitude and the amount of effort you contribute to meeting your goals largely determine your success.

The reality is that no one is perfect. Along the route to your future, you will make mistakes and you will have moments of failure. You can either let those moments of failure wipe you out and sidetrack you, or you can choose to learn from what went wrong and ensure that it does not happen again.

Take for example a certain man who encountered more than his fair share of difficulties. He lost his job, the business he started failed, the love of his life died tragically, he suffered a nervous breakdown, and he was defeated more than four times while running for elected office — and these are just some of his great failures. Many would have said he should have given up along the way. Instead, he kept going and went on to become the man who some credit as one of the greatest presidents of the United States: Abraham Lincoln. The next time you feel defeated by a setback, take into consideration the story of the man who gave the Gettysburg Address.

The most important thing to keep in mind when failure strikes is not the failure, but regrouping your efforts to concentrate on the goal ahead. Mistakes are simply part of the process toward getting what you want; they are not the end result.

Furthermore, eliminate negative people from your dreams and plans for the future. As you are on your way to success, there will be people who tell you that you will not be able to accomplish your goals. These people's thoughts and opinions need to play a very limited role in your life. Surround yourself with people who will encourage you and support you in your endeavors, which can include your friends and family. Sometimes, it is a good idea to find a person to serve as a role model, as you have already seen the benefit of having a positive role model in your child's life. Search out someone who has had success in the goal you are pursuing. Ask them to come alongside you to serve as a mentor or encourager. Not only will he or she be able to guide you, but he or she will be able to offer support that only someone familiar with your goal can provide.

Success, Imagination, Perspiration

If you have not heard this old adage, it serves repeating: Success requires 90 percent perspiration and 10 percent imagination. You will not achieve your goals simply with good intentions and great ideas; it takes hard work and lots of it. There are no easy roads to achieving your goals. As you are working hard, keep in mind your children will be seeing your perseverance and your determination, and you will serve as a role model for them and for what they can achieve.

If you admit defeat and quit, your children will see this and take it as an acceptable way to deal with defeat. When you show your children it is all right to quit, they will learn by example that hard work is worth forsaking when the going gets tough. While living your life as a beacon may seem weighty, it is exactly what a mother must do. So, when you consider giving up, keep in mind that it is not only hopes and dreams that you will be forsaking but your children's as well.

Keep working. Keep planning. Keep dreaming. You can have it all. The future — yours and your child's — is entirely up to you.

Conclusion

Single Mothers' Words of Wisdom

The day that I brought my son home from the hospital, my grandmother offered me some words of great wisdom. Admittedly, after having carried my son for 17 days past his due date, I found her words hard to take to heart at the time. My grandmother said, "Enjoy these moments because this time will all go very quickly."

Now, as the days count down to my son turning 21, I am reminded of those very words. As single mothers, we are often overwhelmed by circumstances and the details of daily living. However, these are not as important as putting aside what we are in the midst of doing when our child wants to show us the bug he just caught or to throw a football in the backyard. I know my son will not remember if the house was vacuumed or if the furniture was dust free, but he most certainly remembers when I stopped what I was doing to watch a sports highlight on ESPN with him or the time we took a walk in the rain without an umbrella. He most certainly still brings to my attention that, despite a hectic writing schedule, I was on the sidelines of most every game he played.

There is no recapturing the moments of our child's growing up; we must simply capture them as they occur. They are irreplaceable snapshots. Capture them and hold them in your heart. They are yours to be treasured. Why? Because you are a child's mother.

~ Janis Adams

Make sure to find time for yourself while still putting your child's needs before your own. Your child needs you to be his or her protector and to be a consistent person in their life.

~Tara Surowiec

Take time to get know yourself. Then, get to know each of your children as individuals. God has given each of your children specifically to you to grow them to be something good in this world. One day, I want to be able to stand before God, and I want to see that He is proud of what I did in their lives.

Always remember the saying life will never give you more than you can handle. So, before saying that your life is too much for you to bear, find out how you are missing the solution that most certainly exists. Many times along the way, I found that most of my problems really were me. Not my kids or my circumstances. The problems were things that I could change myself.

~Helena Grant

Give your children as much stability, encouragement, and love as you can. Let them know that they are important to you and that you will always think of them first. Do not go to court unless you have to; try to work out any situations that might arise between you and your child's father. Most important, keep your children from being placed in the middle of any situations. Being a single mother can be stressful, but do not place that stress on your child and do not let that stress be a part of their daily life.

~Colene Carpenter

Stay strong for yourself and for your children. It is the only way you will make it through. Never argue with your child's father in front of your children. It will hurt them more than you will ever know, now and in the future.

~Dana Castaneda

Family is everything. Keep your family in your life; they have been there from the beginning and always will be a part of you and your children. Go to school and do something with yourself. Follow your dreams, not just for yourself but as an example for your children to one day follow in their own lives.

~Brenda L. Mehrkar-Asl

As a single mother, you must know your child is not automatically "messed up" because you are a single parent. While not an ideal situation, it is very possible to raise healthy, well-adjusted children.

~Heidi Colonna

It is a great challenge to be a single mother, but it will help you develop great skills as a woman that you would never have developed otherwise. Single mothering will make you a stronger woman. You will become persistent, determined, compassionate toward others, motivated, as well as a person who is willing to seek out the services you need and someone who is not willing to give up. It will take time, but over the years, you will see that your investment pays off in the beautiful child you have raised who has turned out to be a healthy adult. You are not alone; there are many people out there who are willing to help.

~Scherry Marie Brady

You need to know without question that you self-worth does not depend on what some guy does or doesn't think of you.

The next thing is enjoy this time of singleness — no matter how long it lasts — with your kids, when it is just you and them.

Last, this came from my mom who was a single mom, "You can either sink or swim, and sinking is not an option."

~Keiran Ross

Appendix A:

Pregnancy Preparedness Checklist

With all the things you will need to do to be prepared for your baby's arrival, it is best to get started early. For some mothers, nine months seems like not enough time to be fully prepared.

Pregnancy Checklist

During the first few weeks of pregnancy:

- ☐ Make an appointment with an ob/gyn as soon as you are aware of your pregnancy
- ☐ Cut out cocktails, caffeine, and stop smoking
- ☐ Avoid sushi, deli meat, soft serve ice cream, and fish with a high level of mercury, for example canned tuna
- ☐ Check cosmetics, skin, and hair care products to see if you discontinue using them during pregnancy (some products are absorbed through your skin and are harmful to the baby)

☐ Begin taking pre-natal vitamins and folic acid

During the second trimester:

☐ Interview day care facilities. Here are some questions you can ask:
  ☐ Is the facility licensed and accredited?
  ☐ Has a criminal check been run on all employees?
  ☐ Are employees trained in infant and child CPR?
  ☐ Do you agree with the caretaking and discipline approach of the center?
  ☐ Are there enough toys, beds, and space for the number of children attending the center?
  ☐ Do the kids attending the center seem happy and well-adjusted?

During the second and third trimester:

☐ Begin to consider baby names
☐ Find a pediatrician
☐ Begin acquiring the following items:
  ☐ Diapers
  ☐ Baby wipes
  ☐ Burp clothes
  ☐ Diaper cream
  ☐ Pacifiers
  ☐ Breast pump
  ☐ Bottles
  ☐ Bottle brush for cleaning
  ☐ Baby nail clipper
  ☐ Breast pads

☐ Nipple cream
☐ Baby shampoo
☐ Baby wash
☐ Baby lotion
☐ Crib sheets/bassinet sheets
☐ Waterproof mattress pad
☐ Onesies
☐ Sleepers
☐ Bibs
☐ Crib bumper
☐ Car seat
☐ Infant seat
☐ Ivory Snow or Dreft for doing baby's laundry. These are the most popular brands; however, there are other brands that offer detergent specifically for baby.

During the third trimester:

☐ Register for baby gifts
☐ Pre-register at the hospital for admittance
☐ Attend childbirth classes
☐ If working, finalize maternity leave
☐ Pack a hospital bag. Your bag should contain the following items:
    ☐ Camera
    ☐ Hospital registration paper work (make sure to complete all forms in advance)
    ☐ Driver's license (you will need it upon admission to the hospital)

- ☐ List of phone numbers of people/family you will want to call upon the birth of the baby
- ☐ Comfortable pajamas (choose something with a button down top for easy access if you plan to nurse. Top and bottom sets seem to work better than gown — make sure the bottom is loose in the event of a C-section)
- ☐ Slippers
- ☐ Robe
- ☐ Nursing bra
- ☐ Nursing pads
- ☐ Sanitary pads (the hospital will supply them, but every girl has her favorites. The hospital size of your favorite brand is suggested as your flow can be quite heavy in the days following the birth. Remember, you cannot use tampons immediately following the baby's birth.)
- ☐ Toiletries — tooth brush, tooth paste, shampoo, lotion, deodorant, make-up
- ☐ Going home outfit (keep in mind the clothes that you wore at about 6 months pregnant will probably be most comfortable; in the case of a C-section, bring very loose clothing)
- ☐ At least $20 in cash for incidentals like food or TV rentals (do not bring much more than this as theft is a problem in some hospitals)
- ☐ Cell phone and charger
- ☐ Baby's coming home outfit
- ☐ Blanket for baby
- ☐ Hat for baby

Getting you pantry/kitchen ready

☐ Make a few meals ahead of time and freeze them. This way you will have meals on hand so that you will not have to cook if you do not feel up to it.

☐ Stock you pantry with necessities. Necessities will include the things that you use regularly that are non-perishable. For example, juices, pasta, spaghetti sauce, and other ingredients for meals that can be easily made without a trip to the grocery store. It is also a good idea to stock up on toilet paper and paper towels as you will need plenty with a newborn.

☐ Get a few take-out menus from your favorite places so you can easily order dinner if you need to. (Check ahead to see if the restaurant delivers, as well.)

Additional tips:

☐ Practice using your car seat. Sometimes the fasteners can be a bit tricky, and it is better to become familiar using them before the baby arrives than to have a cry-ing baby stuck in the seat while you try to learn how to use the fastener. Additionally, it is a good idea to have a police officer or fireman check the seat to confirm that it is correctly installed; most departments offer a time once a month when they offer free evaluations.

☐ Set up the baby's crib prior to the birth so there will be no hassles to contend with when you bring baby home. As well, if you need any spare parts or find you cannot fit the crib together on your own, you can get help before your baby comes home.

☐ Set up a changing area prior to the baby's arrival so that you can make sure that you will have all the items you will need readily available. There is nothing worse than a crying baby with a wet diaper and no wipes available.

☐ Make room for all the baby supplies before you need them so you will feel more organized. Realize, however, that you may want to make changes as to where things are and go as you discover what works best and is most convenient for you and your new little one.

Most important of all, remember this should be a joyful experience. So instead of feeling stressed, choose to be excited and enjoy all the preparations. This is a very special time as you prepare for your baby.

Appendix B:

Resources

Opportunities to connect and exchange information with other mothers

- CafeMom (**www.cafemom.com**) — A site that offers a free forum for mothers to share information, play games, and talk.

- The National Organization of Single Mothers (**www.singlemothers.org**) — This site is dedicated to helping single mother's address their specific daily challenges. Everything from practical advice to emotional support is offered.

- Moms Network (**www.momsnetwork.com**) — Moms Network offers a place for working moms to network. Job site suggestions, work at home opportunities, and home business plans are also offered here.

- Directory for Moms (**http://momz.com/directory-for-moms**) — This site offers a directory of websites specifically addressing the needs of a mother.

- Single Mothers By Choice (**www.singlemothersby-choice.com**) — This website offers advice and direction for any woman considering becoming a single mother or for those women who already single moms by choice. This site offers information on local chapters of the organization and contact information, along with blogs and advice for mothers at any stage of the process.

Opportunities for Support

- Parents Without Partners (**www.parentswithoutpartners.org**) — A national organization that offers support for mothers and fathers who are raising children on their own. The group offers support and activities for both parents and children.

- Single Parents Online Network (**www.singleparentsonline.net**) — An online network offered for both single mothers and fathers.

Adoption options, resources, and advice

- Adoptive Families Magazine (**www.adoptivefamilies.com**) — This site is hosted by the national magazine Adoptive Families. It offers information on adoption and for those in each stage of the process of adoption. It also will direct visitors to other helpful resources for adoptive families.

- National Council for Adoption (**www.ncfa-usa.org**) — Provides advocacy and awareness services for those involved in any part of the adoption process.

Career counseling, educational resources, and job strategies

- College Degree Network (**www.collegedegreenetwork. com**) — This site provides up-to-date information on online degree programs.

- CareerCounseling.com (**www.careercounseling.com**) — Offers a roadmap to success in any chosen career. The site includes résumé services, profiles of employers, job search coaching, and help with finding the right job.

- Ready Minds (**www.readyminds.com**) — Custom career counseling for both the career seeker and the career changer.

Coping with divorce and suggestions for therapy

- American Association for Marriage and Family Therapy (**www.aamft.org**) — Provides area specific aid to locating the right counselor for specific needs and situations.

- American Academy of Child & Adolescent Psychiatry (**www.aacap.org**) — This side directs visitors to understanding the process of seeking out psychiatric help for children, as well as how to locate a professional who focuses on children's psychiatric issues.

Sons and daughters, how to handle them

- Mayo Clinic (**http://www.mayoclinic.com/health/sex-education/CC00032**) — Advice from physicians on how to discuss sex with your teen.

- WebMD (**www.webmd.com/depression/guide/depression-children**) — This site provides a detailed description of the signs and symptoms of depression in children.

Mommy survival and maintenance

- My Exercise for Women (**www.myexercise-for-woman.com**) — This site provides a complete exercise guide for women, everything from exercises to figuring out your optimum weight and the diet to achieve that weight.

Places to find connections or dating relationships

- SingleParentLove.com (**www.singleparentlove.com**) — An international website that offers a place for single moms and dads to establish friendships or dating relationships.

- SingleParentMeet.com (**www.singleparentmeet.com**) — This is a free website for single moms and dads to connect.

Bibliography

Bach, David. *Smart Women Finish Rich: 9 Steps to Achieving Financial Security and Funding Your Dreams.* Broadway. 2002.

Breitman, Patti and Connie Hatch. *How to Say No Without Feeling Guilty: And Say Yes to More Time, and What Matters Most to You.* Broadway. 2001.

Callaway, Phil. Parenting: *Don't Try This at Home: What I Learned While My Kids Were Raising Me.* Harvest House. 2006.

Eller, T. Suzanne. *The Mom I Want to Be: Rising Above Your Past to Give Your Kids a Great Future.* Harvest House. 2006.

Engber, Andrea and Leah Klungness, Ph.D. *The Complete Single Mother: Reassuring Answers to Your Most Challenging Concerns.* Adams Media. 2006.

Evans, Carol. *This Is How We Do It: The Working Mothers' Manifesto*. Hudson Street Press. 2006.

Foley, Jacqueline. *Flex Time: A Working Mother's Guide to Balancing Career and Family*. De Capo Press. 2003.

Hannon, Kerry. *Suddenly Single: Money Skills for Divorces and Widows*. Wiley. 1998.

Hunter, Deedra. *Winning Custody: A Woman's Guide to Retaining Custody of Her Children*. St. Martin's Griffin. 2001.

Livingston, Carole. *Why Was I Adopted?*. Lyle Stuart. 2000.

Munroe, Myles. *Waiting and Dating: A Sensible Guide to a Fulfilling Love Relationship*. Destiny Image. 1998.

Murkoff, Heidi and Sharon Mazel. *What to Expect When You're Expecting: Fourth Edition*. Workman Publishing Company. 2008.

Parrott, Les. *7 Secrets Of A Healthy Dating Relationship*. Beacon Hill Press. 1995.

Schlessinger, Laura. *Stop Whining, Start Living*. Harper Paperbacks. 2008.

Schneider, Meg F. and Joan Zuckerberg. *Difficult Questions Kids Ask and Are Afraid to Ask About Divorce*. Morning Glory Press. 1996.

Tatelbaum, Judy. *The Courage to Grieve: The Classic Guide to Creative Living, Recovery, and Growth Through Grief.* Perennial Library. 1984.

Tatelbaum, Judy. *You Don't Have To Suffer: A Handbook for Transforming Life's Crises.* AuthorHouse. 2005.

Wallen, Jacqueline. *Balancing Work and Family.* Allyn & Bacon. 2001.

Watnik, Webster. *Child Custody Made Simple: Understanding the Law of Child Custody and Child Support.* Single Parent Press. 1996.

Yates, Cynthia. *Living Well as a Single Mom: A Practical Guide to Managing Your Money, Your Kids and Your Personal Life.* Harvest House. 2006.

Author Biography

Janis Adams writes the long-running newspaper column "Saving Grace." She has developed a dedicated following through her wisdom, wit, and insight. Her feature articles have appeared in numerous magazines, newspapers, and journals.

For more information on Adams, her next book, or to schedule an appearance by her, visit **www.janisadams.org**.

Author Janis Adams

Index

S

T

V

W

MORE GREAT PARENTING TITLES

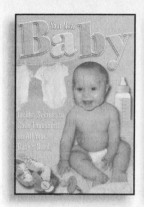 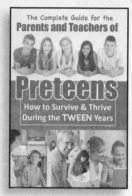 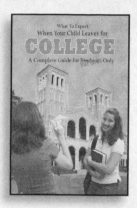

Your New Baby: *Insider Secrets to Save Thousands on All Your Baby's Needs*
This exhaustively researched book will arm you with hundreds of innovative ideas and resources to save you money. Baby items can be quite costly. Knowing exactly what you need to buy and keeping a budget is critical. You will learn many ways that you can get everything you need for the baby safely and on a limited budget.
ISBN-13: 978-1-60138-138-5 • 288 Pgs • $24.95 • SPRING 2008 RELEASE

A Complete Guide for the Parents and Teachers of Preteens: *How to Survive & Thrive During the Tween Years*
This well-researched, extensive guide is for adults who deal with children ages 9 to 12 (tweens). Learn ways to relate to and effectively communicate with children of this age and pave the way for a successful transition to the teen years.
ISBN-13: 978-1-60138-573-4 • 288 Pgs • $24.95 • 2011 RELEASE

What to Expect When Your Child Leaves for College: *A Complete Guide for Parents Only*
This book provides you with valuable information and will help make the college transition easier. You will learn how to encourage independence, how to offer support, how to handle the drop-off, how to deal with empty nest syndrome, how to talk to your child about his or her emotions, how to plan meaningful family time, and how to teach your child to live on his or her own.
ISBN-13: 978-1-60138-218-4 • 288 Pgs • $21.95 • 2008 RELEASE

MORE GREAT PARENTING TITLES

A Complete Guide for Single Dads: *Everything You Need to Know About Raising Healthy, Happy Children on Your Own*

Through hours of meticulous research and interviews, this book was compiled to show exactly how a single father can raise a child alone to be happy and healthy without the help of a second parent. You will learn, as a single father, how to reassure your children and maintain the feeling of a family. You will learn how to help them feel better regardless of whether you are a single father through death or divorce. You will learn how to treat your children and how to communicate with them. The basics of discipline and rules will be outlined for a single-parent household, along with tips on how you can have fun with your children the right and healthy way. You will learn the differences between having daughters versus sons as a father, and how to handle the myriad issues that the mothaer would normally handle. For every father alone for the first time or unsure of how to raise a child alone, this book will provide the detailed instruction you need to be the best possible single father.

ISBN 13: 978-1-60138-396-9 • 288 Pgs • $24.95 • 2011 RELEASE

Your Child's First Pet: *A Parent's Guide to Ensuring Success*

This book provides a detailed walkthrough of the best ways to acclimate a child to raising a pet. It will help you choose a pet your child can handle and that will thrive in their care.

ISBN 13: 978-1-60138-394-5 • 288 Pgs • $24.95 • 2011 RELEASE

The Parent's Guide to Uncluttering Your Home: *How to Organize What You Need and Recycle What You Don't*

Learn unique and effective techniques to unclutter your home and keep it that way. This book includes advice and examples for people with children of all ages, plus ways to make organization fun.

ISBN 13: 978-1-60138-338-9 • 288 Pgs • $24.95 • 2011 RELEASE

To order call 1-800-814-1132 or visit www.atlantic-pub.com